You Can Count on Cupid

YOU CAN COUNT ON CUPID

UNCOVERING LOVE BY THE NUMBERS,
FROM THE FIRST DATE, TO THE SEVEN-YEAR ITCH,
TO FOREVER AFTER

Luisa Dillner, MD

A Holt Paperback ◆ Henry Holt and Company ◆ New York

Holt Paperbacks
Henry Holt and Company, LLC
Publishers since 1866
175 Fifth Avenue
New York, New York 10010
www.henryholt.com

Library of Congress Cataloging-in-Publication Data
Dillner, Luisa.
    You can count on cupid : uncovering love by the numbers, from the first
date, to the seven-year itch, to forever after / Luisa Dillner.
        p. cm.
    Includes bibliographical references and index.
    ISBN: 978-0-8050-9041-3
    1. Man-woman relationships. 2. Mate selection. 3. Interpersonal
relations—Research. I. Title.
    HQ801.D558   2010
    646.7'7—dc22   2009011812

Originally published as *Love by Numbers: The Hidden Facts Behind Everyone's
Relationships* in Great Britain in 2009 by Profile Books Ltd., London
First Holt Paperbacks Edition 2010

Designed by Meryl Sussman Levavi
Printed in the United States of America
10 9 8 7 6 5 4 3 2 1

For John, Sam, Madeleine, Mathilda, Lydia, and my mum; all helped me to write this book

Contents

You Can Count on Cupid

Introduction

This isn't a self-help book about relationships, so it won't tell you what to do. What it will do is answer, using facts and figures, from science, sociology, psychology, and a range of other fields, many of the questions people have about relationships; and once you have this information, you can work most things out for yourself.

When I was a single parent with two children, I used to wonder if I'd ever meet someone new. It seemed unlikely, even without taking into account how useless I was (then) at relationships. But one day I came across a newspaper report that said that 70 percent of single parents were likely to find a new mate within five years. I was so surprised that I tore it out. It had never occurred to me that there'd be an answer to the question, Will I meet someone? I'd thought the answer to that question came down to chance, not well-informed prediction. Having prepared myself for years of maternal sacrifice, I found myself thinking I was more likely to meet someone than not. Maybe if the statistics said I would, I didn't even need to try too hard. As it happens, I met my fiancé at a friend's party (a good place, so the research tells us, but I have to thank my friend Janice, who insisted I get out there) and have been with him ever since. Despite my skepticism, I found I could count on cupid after all.

Finding this statistic made me wonder how much research there was about all the eternal, and unusual, questions about relationships: Will I meet someone? Should we move in together? Should I have had that one-night stand? And so on. I'd been working as a doctor, first in hospitals and then for the *British Medical Journal*, and everyone was talking about "evidence-based medicine." There was a big push for doctors to make sure they were treating people on the basis of the best research evidence. If this was such a good thing, why, I wondered, didn't we use it to inform other areas of our lives? When I heard people telling their friends what to do about their boyfriends, husbands, wives, or girlfriends, I couldn't help thinking, But how do you know?

We may think that our feelings about relationships, and especially love, are unique—that no one goes through what we're going through. How we feel about Tom, Dick, or Harriet is sometimes (especially to our friends) inexplicable. But even so, we'll often sound out our friends, who are usually game enough to offer an opinion, based mostly on their sometimes limited experience. What we may not realize is that there are lots of research studies that show what happened to not just a couple of people but sometimes hundreds who have had similar relationship dilemmas to the ones we're having. Research in these areas occasionally makes it into the national press, but the vast majority of similar findings are not known to the public.

When I started writing my column, "Love by Numbers," in London's *Guardian* newspaper, instead of just giving an opinion like traditional advice columns, I wanted to see if I could provide quantitative answers. And looking for research about relationships, I was surprised how much there was—and how quirky some of it was. There is research on whether men will leave their wives for their mistresses (they usually won't), whether open marriages make people happier (they don't), and how often attempts to "poach someone" are successful (around 50 percent of the time). Researchers, mostly social psychologists, have hidden in park bushes to see whether couples without children are more affectionate to each other than lovers encumbered by kids (they are). They have scanned college yearbooks to see whether women who smile in their photos are happier in their relationships than those who don't (they are). And then there are the relationship experts like John M. Gottman, who watches couples in his love lab, identifying precisely the ones most likely to split up by listening for just a few minutes to how they talk to each other and applying a mathematical formula.

Some of the conclusions seemed obvious, but most of them were surprising. Perhaps the most surprising thing is that the research, from academic journals (such as the *Journal of Personality and Social Psychology*, the *Journal of Marriage and Family*, and *Sex Roles*), think tanks, government reports, and statistical offices, answers the everyday questions we all have about relationships. Does having children ruin relationships? What's the best way of finding a romantic partner? Do opposites attract? Is there such a thing as a soul mate?

Not all research is created equal; papers vary in quality, and some samples are more representative than others. (Psychologists have a habit of using their students for research, and they are not always like the rest of us.) The research in this book is international, but a lot of it comes from the United States and Britain because many of the research centers and journals are based in these countries. I've tried to include the most useful evidence and to describe any shortcomings it might have. Sometimes the evidence comes from surveys, and it's hard to know who will have taken part. Even the best studies have their limitations, and their findings can only give you more information—not a definitive answer. But often knowing what has happened to other people can shed some light on what might happen to you and what you can do about it.

Many of the letters I get sent for the *Guardian* column are about sex, often from men saying they're not getting enough (which makes you wonder if any men ever do). One letter was from a woman saying that now that she'd had a baby, her husband wanted more sex to make up for the time they'd lost. "I just want to sleep," she wrote. "I don't like to ask what the mothers in playgroup are doing." It's a shame she didn't know, because they're almost certainly doing the same as she is— having less sex than they used to. If men don't ever get enough sex, women don't ever get enough help with child care and the housework. And the two, as we'll see, are related.

People often ask if reconnecting with an ex is likely to work, or if someone who's left them will come back. I used to tell friends that their ex might change his or her mind; now I'd tell them it's pretty unlikely. That's because the research shows that someone who physically leaves a relationship has usually emotionally left it a few months earlier. Some of the letters are sad—why do people have affairs with their romantic partners' best friends?—but most of them are inquiring and optimistic.

I don't get many letters from gay people, which is a pity as there's a growing research base in this area. Some of the research on heterosexuals is applicable to gay relationships, but some research shows that these relationships are different: they tend to be more equal and, for example, use more humor in arguments. As more research is done, we're learning more about the similarities and differences between straight and gay relationships.

The people who write me increasingly ask for facts and figures—I'd be surprised if advice columnists in general get asked for the evidence for their answers—and I have to admit that sifting through the research has made me think I haven't been terribly good at my relationships. There are various habits that are particularly destructive to couples, and I've been guilty of a few of them. I now no longer shriek, "You never do anything around the house!" and instead go for a more gentle, "It would really help me if you could do the vacuuming." I avoid resurrecting fights from five years ago when arguing about something unrelated, and have reluctantly given up nasty name-calling. I try to remember my fiancé is a person too, who has his own hopes and fears, however inconvenient these may be. Sadly, I have realized, relationships are not all about me, after all.

One thing my fiancé and I have always been good at is having a laugh during an argument, which researchers rather pleasingly report is a good thing. Sometimes he'll say, "You're only doing this because you've read some research that says you should." "Well," I reply, "that's a good thing, isn't it?" Once you've read this book, you may want to hide it, to avoid similar accusations.

Mr. or Ms. Right

Pickup Lines

I've never been any good at picking up women. A friend suggested some pickup lines that work for him but sound gross to me. He's very good-looking, so women probably don't care what he's saying. But can pickup lines work, and if so, which ones do work?

There is a science to pickup lines. A pickup line works if it shows you off to some advantage, by making you look interesting, humorous, athletic, or rich. Preferably all of the above. The risk is that the wrong line, even if delivered by a Brad Pitt lookalike, will be met with ridicule. The type of ridicule that can haunt you forever. But on the bright side, there are tips to be had, because there's been research on the best pickup lines. Questions seem to work better than statements. A study of one hundred people (ranging in age from twenty-two to forty-five years) who went on three-minute speed dates were asked to pick the best opening lines they heard. The researchers, from the University of Hertfordshire in England, were generous enough to share the results. The winning pickup line? "What is your favorite pizza topping?" Lines like this are open questions that give the other person the chance to respond in a lighthearted way, something that the worst pickup lines ("I have a PhD in computer science" and "My best friend is a helicopter pilot") fail to do.

More detailed research into pickup lines has been undertaken based on hypothetical stories. A study of 205 undergraduates by psychologists at the University of Edinburgh in Scotland asked them to rank pickup lines from made-up scenarios. Women liked the one where a man at a trendy bar says, "I'm one of the owners here, would you like to dance?" thus showing off his wealth and dancing ability, two highly desirable qualities, in one sentence. The use of these scenarios may bias the study, however. In one of them, in which a man protects a woman from two larger louts, you'd have to think any pickup line would be a winner, even "I have a PhD in computer science."

Men, bless them, like to use sexual pickup lines, as in "If I said you had a beautiful body, would you hold it against me?" and "I may not be Fred Flintstone, but I bet I could make your Bed Rock," or the even less poetic "Is there a mirror in your undies? I think I can see myself in them." This, the research tells us, is their subtle way of finding a woman who wants to get laid. Women say they prefer pickup lines that show a man could have more long-term potential. Therefore any opening line that shows off wealth (which studies show is something women still find strangely appealing in a mate), a generous nature, and confidence (in a realistic way, so not "Shall I buy you an island?") is attractive. Empty compliments don't seem to work, although lines such as "Was your father a thief? He must have stolen the stars to put them in your eyes" or "If you were a tear in my eye, I wouldn't cry for fear of losing you" have a cheesy charm.

Whatever pickup line you use, make sure that you smile when you say it. Smiling increases your chances of a positive response, and some people will make up their mind about you before you've opened your mouth.

Online Mating

Is Internet dating a good way to meet someone? I haven't had a relationship with anyone since I broke up with my boyfriend three years ago. I don't want to be on my own, and online dating seems more acceptable than it used to be. How successful is it likely to be? I'm thirty-five years old.

The Internet is one of the most common ways for people to find dates. A Nielsen/NetRatings survey on meeting people ranked it third after "through friends" and "in pubs and clubs" and estimated that 3.5 million people a month use dating Web sites. Around 11 percent of us who use the Internet visit a dating site each month. And why not? You can do it from home (initially), twenty-four hours a day (if you have the stamina), it's relatively safe and anonymous (if you're careful), and no longer just for those who are desperate. It's now almost cool to find your true love online. And although some people sign up to find "friends" and have flings, a Pew Internet Study in the United States of over three thousand adults found that 15 percent knew someone in a long-term relationship that had started online and that 17 percent of people had married someone they had first met online. The survey estimated that approximately 16 million Americans have gone to a dating Web site to meet people online. Match.com says that two hundred thousand people a month find someone on its site.

A more academically robust study of 229 online daters by Dr. Jeff Gavin of Bath University in England showed that on average most significant online relationships lasted for seven months, with a quarter lasting a year. Gavin says that success rates are similar to offline methods but that the opportunity for people to remain anonymous for a while is an advantage. People feel they can express their emotions more readily online, which can accelerate intimacy. On the other hand, people can also lie more easily since they don't have to show their face or figure. Studies show that people most commonly lie about weight, age, and, oh yes, being married. Some lie more spectacularly. Karen Carlton, a divorcee in Fife, Scotland, lived for two years with a former U.S. marine she met online, before she found out he was a fabulist from Leicester, in central England.

If you have reasonable expectations, online dating is a good way to start looking for dates. Sensible precautions apply, as they do in offline life: don't give away too much information about yourself, meet in a public place (lunch at a restaurant is good, as you can get away in just over an hour if you've had enough), choose profiles with photos. Beware of men who only "wink" at you on sites (time wasters), call themselves "Top Gun," or e-mail "My life was meaningless without you; I think of you every minute of every day" within the first week, since this is not normal behavior. Increase your success rate by posting a photo and a truthful profile. Online dating agencies advise looking friendly rather than seductive or moody in photos, as approachability increases success rates. Best of all, use a dictionary when composing your profile. One of the biggest turnoffs, apparently, is a profile with poor spelling.

Speedy Dating

> I'm twenty-six years old and broke up with my girl-
> friend eight months ago. Since then I've been single.
> I've considered speed dating, but I'm worried that
> no one will choose to see me again. Is there any-
> thing I can do to increase my chances of success?

One of the joys of speed dating is that it protects you from instant rejection. No woman will dismiss you to your face. You
usually only hear if you've had any matches (if someone you
want to see also wants to see you again) a couple of days after
the event. And you should get at least one match at an event.
Ever since Rabbi Yaacov Deyo invented speed dating in Los
Angeles in 1998 to help Jewish singles get together, it has been
frequently studied. Most speed daters haven't met each other
before—so these are random meetings, albeit among people
who select themselves by choosing to go speed dating—and
by finding out how speed daters choose each other, researchers
can work out what attracts people to each other. At least, that
is, at a speed-dating event. As you'll see, a speed date is not so
different from a regular first date—just even more superficial.

So prepare to be underwhelmed. To be successful, you'll
need to be tall, young, slim, and good-looking. A recent study
from Essex University in England of 3,600 men and women
attending speed-dating events found that every one inch of
height a man had over other men increased his chances of being picked by 5 percent. In studies of what people look for in
long-term partners, they'll say "kindness, intelligence, and an
attractive personality." Well, speed daters leave some of that
touchy-feely stuff at home. The three- or four-minute time
limit on each date means that market forces apply. Education

and income have little influence, although other studies show that thin, tall people are more likely to have higher incomes. About two-thirds of speed daters in the studies have college degrees; the U.S. national average is 28 percent according to U.S. census data. A study in *Evolution and Human Behavior* of over 10,500 Americans who took part in HurryDate sessions also found that both sexes cared most about physical appearance and that few people were picked on the basis of their income, personality, or wealth.

Be warned that women are choosier than men. In the study of HurryDate sessions, women chose two to three men per session and saw 45 percent of their choices matched. Men chose five women and had 20 percent matched. A third of men but only 11 percent of women got no matches. Many people don't choose anyone; those who think they are less desirable may pick more people as matches to increase their chances of getting a date with someone.

How successful speed dating is at generating long-term relationships is less clear because these studies have yet to be done, but a study from Northwestern University published in *Personal Relationships* found that 163 undergraduate speed daters embarked on over five hundred dates afterward. Not exactly long-term follow-up, but it shows enthusiasm.

As in all markets, your success depends on the competition. If you wear shoe lifts, hold in your stomach, look young, and have a nice, friendly face, you'll get lots of interest. Your personality will only matter on the dates that, it is hoped, follow.

Romantic Timing

I'm a single forty-something male who recently joined a dating Web site. After an indifferent start I was told by a female friend that women are not interested in beginning new relationships in the winter and that spring is the best time for this. Is this true? Or are relationships more likely to begin at a different time of the year?

Spring always feels like such a hopeful season, doesn't it? So full of promise. Yet strangely it doesn't feature as a peak time of activity for dating Web sites. The most popular times for people to sign up with dating services are January, February (in the aftermath of a barren Valentine's Day), and the second week of September, says Mary Balfour, managing director of the dating agency Drawing Down the Moon. Balfour believes that the peaks reflect people's needs to reassess their relationship status shortly after Christmas (no one to kiss under the mistletoe) and at the end of summer (after ill-judged holiday romances). Match.com (20 million members worldwide) says its busiest day ever was January 6, 2008, reflecting a rush of New Year's resolutions to find a mate. But the evidence is conflicting; a survey by ComScore, Inc., found a peak in online dating sites in the United States in July.

Hard times seem to drive people to dating sites and agencies whatever the month. An article in the *Los Angeles Times* claimed that both eHarmony and Match.com reported especially high traffic on days when the Dow Jones Industrial Average plummeted.

Balfour's view of spring being the best season to launch an online romantic assault? "It's a load of rubbish." If you've had an indifferent start to online dating, you should blame your profile or photograph rather than the season. Photographs are essential; you are twelve times more likely to get approached if someone can see what you look like. As already mentioned, try to look friendly rather than moodily handsome, and while

13

we're at it, your profile should be flirty (not sleazy) and humorous. If you regularly update your profile, it moves you up
the search-engine hierarchy, so more people will find you.
There's apparently a shortage of single men in their forties, so
rather than wait for lambs to gambol in the fields and daffodils
to bloom, just make sure you come across as half decent and
sane.

That you shouldn't wait for spring is further (if weakly)
backed up by a survey of more than one thousand people by
the Scripps Howard News Service. Over half of the people in
this survey thought spring no more romantic than any other
season, though men were slightly more dewy-eyed about it.
There's an argument that December, with its lack of day-
light and the magic of Christmas, is the most romantic month,
which is borne out by the fact that it usually has the highest
rates of conception, although there are also less romantic ex-
planations for this assessment, involving alcohol and unpro-
tected sex.

Social anthropologists theorize that autumn should be
the peak time to try to find a mate, as life goes back to normal
rhythms after the summer holidays and you look for someone
to cook with and snuggle up with under the duvet. Someone
to nest with.

But we don't know when the peak season is for actual success in romance; we only know about when people start trying
to find someone. So if you want a relationship, you shouldn't
wait for some optimum time that doesn't exist. The reality is
that clocks have little to do with it. Whatever the time zone,
what matters is that the timing's right for both you and the
other party.

In the Stars?

> I'm a twenty-eight-year-old man who is having a great relationship with a lovely woman for the first time in five years. The only problem is that she's into horoscopes—she reads them every day. She's delighted that our signs are compatible, but I wonder if she would be so keen if they weren't. There is no evidence that your sign determines who you are attracted to, is there?

The short answer is no, don't be absurd. But there's a longer one, too, because horoscopes are sufficiently irritating to provoke researchers into providing evidence to disprove them. Which is just as well because many people believe them. According to a 2004 survey of three thousand young people between the ages of eighteen and twenty-four reported in London's *Guardian* newspaper, two-thirds of respondents believed in horoscopes, a figure that is not far behind the 78 percent of Americans who told the Pew Research Center that they believe in the Bible. A survey of 1,122 art students and 383 science students at York University in Toronto found that 92 percent knew their star sign. (What planet had the others been on? Even my seven-year-old daughter knows she's a Leo.) In the same survey, a quarter of the art students and one in five science students said they had made a conscious decision based on their horoscope in the past year. Since horoscopes are vague, as in "Be careful what you wish for; being wealthy does not necessarily bring happiness," one wonders what decisions they made. A study by the French statistician Michel Gauquelin involved sending a description of the personality characteristics in the astrological sign for one of the worst mass murderers in French history to 150 people and asked how well it fitted them; 94 percent said they recognized themselves in the description.

It is clearly annoying to think you have been chosen for your star sign, but since 500 million people share that sign, you can still take some personal credit. If someone truly believes that as a Pisces they are best off with a Scorpio, they may look out for or at least be receptive to people with that star sign. But any activity along these lines is marginal. A study by Dr. David Voas at the University of Manchester in England analyzed the birthdays of 20 million husbands and wives using data from the 2001 UK census. It found no evidence that astrological signs had any impact on the probability of marrying someone of any other sign. If there had been even a small influence, such as one in one thousand influenced by the stars, he calculated we would see ten thousand more couples than expected with certain combinations of star signs. But there weren't. Astrologers criticized his study for not looking at full birth charts (with birth dates and times), but, as Voas says, he used the same criteria as are used in astrologers' columns. Perhaps most interesting was that Voas found a random distribution of birthday combinations—so that even a belief in astrology didn't influence people in their marriage choices.

If your only problem with your girlfriend is that she believes in horoscopes, things are going pretty well and you can rest easy in the knowledge that whatever she thinks, your star sign is not what makes you compatible. The only thing I'd be worried about is what else your girlfriend believes in. Check out where she stands on dragons and flying saucers.

Birth Order

> I am the oldest child in my family, and my boyfriend is the youngest in his. I have heard that the order in which you are born into your family influences your personality, who would be your ideal mate, and even if you become gay. Is there anything in this?

Birth order does have an influence on personality and behavior, but the question is, How much? Parents treat their oldest and youngest children differently—with the latter getting more relaxed upbringings. According to Dr. Kevin Leman, a psychologist with a research interest in birth order, firstborns are natural leaders, who take responsibility, are more likely to have fewer sexual partners, and fully commit to making relationships work. An Australian parenting expert, Michael Grose, says that every male U.S. astronaut has been the eldest child or firstborn boy in the family as have more than half of American presidents. Firstborns are also overrepresented in boardrooms. Vistage, the world's largest organization of chief executives, carried out a survey for *USA Today* and found that out of 1,582 responses, 43 percent of the CEOs were born first in their family and 23 percent were born last (leaving 33 percent somewhere in the middle).

Firstborns are, it is said, the ones most likely to marry their childhood sweethearts. This conformity, however, makes them less spontaneous (for that read "dull in bed") but committed to going the distance. Now, the good news for you is that their best match is with a youngest child. This is because youngest children are fun (they got to go out all night because their parents were too worn out to argue) and loving (they received more cuddles), but they appreciate the parental qualities that firstborns often possess. Younger children can have issues of laziness—because they're accustomed to having everything done for them. But then oldest children have control issues (so it's a stalemate when two firstborns get together). Middle children work hard at relationships (they tend to compromise), and twins make understanding mates because they've always had someone else to think about. Children without brothers and sisters are super dependable and supportive.

However much we might recognize some of these personality traits, we're as likely to think of just as many exceptions to these rules, and the research doesn't back up some of the traits. A study of 438 men and women by researchers at Florida Atlantic University and published in the journal *Personality and Individual Differences* found that firstborns had more sexual partners than later-born children. In support of the commitment theory of firstborns, they wanted children at a younger age than those lower down in birth order. But there were no differences in when first- and later-born children settled down in long-term relationships.

There is considerable research looking at birth order and sexual preference. A study of over 87,000 men and 71,000 women by researchers at the University of Toronto, done through a BBC Internet survey, found that having older brothers increased the likelihood of a man being homosexual—but specifically for men who were not right-handed (so for those who were either left-handed or ambidextrous). Each older brother, the study found, increased the likelihood of being homosexual by 15 percent. Birth order had no effect on women's sexuality.

However strong or weak the effect of birth order on relationships, there isn't much you can do about it. Nothing, actually. And using "What's your birth order?" as a pickup line is as bad as asking someone about his or her star sign.

Wanted: Handsome Men

I have been looking for a relationship for some time, but I don't meet many men whom I find that good-looking, and looks are important to me. I see many more good-looking women than men. This isn't just because I think the women I know are attractive but because I know their personalities. And I do care about men's personalities, too. But do men have more choice when it comes to good-looking romantic partners?

The short answer to your question, which runs the risk of sexual stereotyping, is that women may still make more of an effort to appear attractive when they go out and hence seem better looking.

However, evolutionary psychologists (who research how evolution might have made us how we are) think there's some evidence that there really are more beautiful women than gorgeous men in the world. This fits with the Trivers-Willard hypothesis, beloved of evolutionary psychologists, that says parents who have any inheritable trait that is good for a particular sex will have more surviving children (and grandchildren) of that sex. Robert Trivers, an evolutionary biologist, and Dan Willard, a mathematician, reckoned that tall, strong fathers would have more sons because hunter-gatherers did better against wild bison if they were bigger. Sons can also have more children (they don't have to deal with the nine-months-of-pregnancy bit) and spread these desirable genes. Women who are young, not too tall, have symmetrical facial features, and carry a reasonably healthy body weight (women forever get it wrong about men wanting size zero girlfriends) are more likely to have girls because these factors are associated with fertility. And fertility is a woman's greatest asset, evolutionarily speaking. In short, men look for above average in looks and average in other traits for long-term partners. Women (and I am just repeating the body of evidence) go for looks more in the short term and money (as well as good communication skills and a sense of humor) over the long term.

In a study of three thousand Americans from the Longitudinal Study of Adolescent Health by Satoshi Kanazawa of the London School of Economics, the attractiveness of parents was rated on a five-point scale. (There is evidence that there is a lot of global agreement on what constitutes good looks.) He found that parents rated "very attractive" were 26 percent less likely to have a son, having taken other factors such as education and number of sexual partners into account. What this means, of course, is that if better-looking people have more daughters than sons, women will continue to get better looking while men, well, won't. But men may think they are good-looking anyway. In the study, 28 percent of the sample rated themselves as "very attractive," whereas only 11 percent were so rated by the researcher.

This study has been criticized on statistical grounds for being more speculative than scientifically proven, and there are many people who sniff at evolutionary psychology. But feel free to take this as some evidence that you're right. However, looks are only part of what's attractive about someone. There are many other psychological studies that support the more developed view that if you like someone's personality you'll rate them as better looking. So you could try that too and see if it works.

Reeling from Rejection

I'm twenty-six years old and ready to embark on a serious, fulfilling relationship with a man. I am a very passionate person and cannot hold back when I really feel for someone. I've recently met a man who has bowled me over to the extent that if we had a relationship and it were to fail in the near future, I don't think I would recover for a few months, especially if he rejected me. This has caused me to consider whether I am not the kind of person who is able to have relationships at all.

It's normal to be a bit scared of getting hurt by a relationship, but not if you are so terrified that you'd rather not risk one at all. Getting dumped is an almost universal experience, and most people bounce back, believing that things will work out with someone else. (A few months isn't so long, actually.) If you are oversensitive to rejection, you may take being dumped too personally and assume that anyone you get involved with will also dump you. And hey, let's not stop there—maybe no one likes you. You'll end up working from the premise that to know you is not to like you, which ends up being a self-fulfilling prophecy. Instead you need to believe, as most people do, that next time it will be different.

Psychologists say that our ability to deal with rejection is based on how we learn to attach ourselves to people, mostly as children. If you have a fearful attachment style, you will be overly anxious that closeness leads to rejection. This is not good for your mental health. A study by Professor Toni Bifulco at the University of London asked 222 women who had been identified as having a higher risk than normal of depression by their family doctor to fill out a questionnaire on attachment style based on a global scale. Bifulco found that those with fearful attachment styles were nearly three times more likely to become depressed within twelve months than those with "secure" attachment styles. So you need to find ways to stop feeling like this, as it's destructive.

Other studies show that if you are sensitive to rejection you will trash your relationships, seeing rejection where it doesn't exist and driving your significant other bonkers by overreacting to perceived slights. People who are preoccupied with being rejected tend to be unhappier in relationships because they expect them to end and are anxious, jealous, and controlling—all recognized ways of tipping relationships into oblivion. You can get professional help—cognitive behavioral therapy may help you think more positively about yourself and your relationships, for example—but you can start with friends you can trust, checking your view of reality against their view. Then you can reset your sensitivity gauge. Since you don't know this man very well yet, why not reset your passion gauge as well? You can't really be mad about someone before you get to know them. So in the interests of self-preservation, tread more cautiously.

Nice Guy But . . .

I'm not successful with women, although I've got many female friends. The women I want to go out with seem to prefer men who treat them badly. My friends say I'm too nice. Don't women want to date nice guys?

What is a nice guy? In various studies women define nice men as anything from kind, considerate, and loyal to passive, sexually inexperienced, and boring. Women also use "too nice" euphemistically, to reject men they really think are too dull. Women do want to date nice guys, when "nice" means something attractive, but the studies supporting this statement are not that helpful. They are based on surveys of women who select the characteristics of men they would date rather than those they actually do date. And hypothetical scenarios don't always come that close to real-life reactions.

For example, a study in the journal *Sex Roles* put three scenarios to forty-eight female undergraduates at a Northeastern private liberal arts college. Their average age was twenty (another limitation). The women had been given scripted answers from hypothetical men to the question, "What is your definition of a real man?" The "nicest" man said he was in touch with his and his mate's feelings, was kind, and put his mate's pleasure in the bedroom first. The "middle" nice one said he was good to the woman he loved. And the third said he didn't go in for touchy-feely stuff. So guess who won? Mr. Nicest was chosen not only as the best boyfriend but as the top husband and platonic friend. When the study used photos of men of varying attractiveness alongside these answers, being good-looking and the nicest man sent his scores through the roof.

But nice men may do less well in the real world because they don't pursue women, won't talk them into a date, and never grab. Many people exaggerate the truth (they stop short of lying) to get themselves a date; a nice guy reduces his chances because he wouldn't dream of cheating in that way. Some men act like they're not that into a woman to keep her interested. This isn't an option for a nice guy because they're just not mean enough.

Nice on its own is not enough; women want good-looking, interesting, fun, and passionate. The amount of niceness that's desirable depends on the vacant position; it's vital for a long-term partner but not essential for a casual fling. Studies show that women prefer risk-taking and unreliable men for short-term relationships. But nice is a great attribute, and you'll get a date eventually. Work on some of the other things that women want, such as being interesting, confident, and making the most of your appearance, and you'll get one even faster.

Blonde or Brunette?

> My friend is blonde, and although we are both quite attractive she gets more attention from men when we go out together. Is it true that gentlemen prefer blondes?

The evidence for whether men prefer blondes is not that robust, coming as it does from evolutionary psychology, which can only provide theories, and research by, for example, City University in London, which, while sound, is funded by Sunsilk, purveyors of fine hair products. You could try watching the classic musical *Gentlemen Prefer Blondes* (originally a novel) starring Jane Russell as the brunette and Marilyn Monroe as the blonde and come to your own conclusions. And think of Barbie—is she a brunette? I don't think so.

We can start with some other research from the City University study in which 468 men were asked to describe the same model, who was wearing digitally enhanced blonde, brown, or red hair. Blonde women were described as less intelligent but more approachable. A total of 53 percent thought most people found blondes more attractive, but they said they themselves had no preference. Out of those who did have a preference, they preferred women to have the same color hair as they did—so blonde men preferred fair-haired women. There may be bias in this study as men may have thought they'd look shallow picking the blonde. But would that worry them? A similar study from the University of Coventry in England asked 120 people to rate a model for characteristics such as intelligence and popularity. The model scored lowest for intelligence when wearing a platinum blonde wig, but she won the popularity vote.

Studies show cultural differences in ideal body shape, but I couldn't find any research specifically looking at hair color in countries other than Western ones. A study in the *Scandinavian Journal of Psychology* of 130 men and 112 women asked the participants to rate twelve drawings of people with varying skin and hair color. Brunettes and fairer-skinned people were rated most highly.

There is an argument, though, that Ice Age man preferred blondes. A paper by the Canadian anthropologist Peter Frost published in the journal *Evolution and Human Behavior* argues that in northern Europe eleven thousand years ago there was a male shortage due to deaths while out hunting. In the scuffle for mates blonde women stood out: there were fewer of them, and their hair shone in the sunlight. And so, Frost says, they were picked more often by men. Frost also cites studies showing that blonde hair darkens more slowly with age and is thus associated with youth and fertility, another reason for the attraction to blondes. So northern Europe developed a diversity of hair (and also eye) color over a relatively short time (conditions were different in other continents). Over twelve pages Frost argues that the MC1R gene for color (which you can't get out of a bottle) is responsible for the variation in Europeans' hair coloring.

So blondes may have had the edge, but the tide has now turned. Worse, there have been media reports quoting the World Health Organization as saying natural blondes are dying out (due to the MC1R gene being a feeble, recessive gene and because men find blondes out of a bottle more attractive than the genuine article). The last blonde was predicted to be born in Finland in 2202. But if you are a bitter brunette (and I'm not saying you are), don't take any comfort from this. It was all a hoax. The WHO even issued what must be its strangest press release. "WHO . . . would like to stress that we have no opinion on the future existence of blondes."

Dim View

> I find guys who wear glasses a bit of a turnoff. I have good eyesight, and I'd like my children to inherit this trait. My heart sinks when I realize a date is wearing contact lenses. I realize I'm cutting down my chances of meeting a soul mate by rejecting the increasing number of men in their thirties who wear glasses. What are the odds my offspring will have good eyesight if my future partner doesn't?

It isn't possible to give exact odds because geneticists think both near- and farsightedness are caused by a combination of oddball genes and environmental factors. A study at St. Thomas' Hospital in London that looked at the DNA of 221 pairs of identical and nonidentical twins found people with myopia (nearsightedness) had faults in the PAX6 gene, which controls how the eye develops. Previous research estimates that inherited factors account for 89 percent of the risk for nearsightedness and the environment accounts for 11 percent. But that won't give your children their personal odds. When my mother said, "Don't sit so close to the TV, it will ruin your eyes," I didn't believe her and thought she was just trying to ruin my life. But it turns out that a child's risk of nearsighted-ness is increased by sitting too close to the TV, playing on game consoles, and even reading too much (although there is no definition of "too much"). In the United States, 30 percent of people are nearsighted, according to the American Opto-metric Association. Don't fall for a Singaporean, as up to 80 percent of young men in Singapore are nearsighted.

But having kids who need glasses is the least of your wor-ries, because there are worse things that can happen to some-one than needing minor visual assistance. If in your survey for a significant other you've got tick boxes that just say "soul mate," "good-looking," "great in bed," and "makes me laugh," your ambition is clearly limited. Why not include "no family history of heart disease, depression, alcoholism, or diabetes"? All these carry an increased risk for your child's long-term health. While you're at it, ask your next boyfriend to draw a family tree to make sure no one's died early from any rare ge-netic disorders. Families sometimes forget that stuff. And why stop there? Whatever happened to screening boyfriends for their earning potential and likelihood of inheriting money? You wouldn't want your children suffering from any diseases caused by poverty.

We are all biologically driven to get the best genes for our kids. Anthropologists cite shiny-haired, slim women as being desirable because they scream, "I've got good genes and can give you perfect healthy babies." But there are no guarantees that any baby you have will be healthy, or that your offspring will grow up untouched by any illness or hardship. Perhaps your wish to screen as much as possible beforehand reflects some deeper anxieties about motherhood. If you don't find men with glasses or contact lenses attractive, so be it. But if you do reject a guy that you like because he is visually chal-lenged, you are the nearsighted one.

Big Egos

> I am attracted to conventionally good-looking men who have large egos, and I worry I will never meet someone with whom I can be in a committed relationship. The men I show an interest in run a mile when they realize I would like something long-term with them. Can men with large egos ever feel love for someone other than themselves?

Most women are attracted to good-looking men—so no mystery there. It's the supersize ego that's the problem. While a strong sense of self is fine, someone bordering on the narcissistic is not well suited to committed relationships. The research shows that people who love themselves too much usually hope there will be someone even better for their image in the next bar, however charming and absorbed in you they seem at the outset. The men you describe (and there are women too) won't modify their behavior in relationships because they can't see what's in it for them. They certainly don't want intimacy. Yuck.

Researchers from the University of Georgia carried out a study to see if narcissistic people ever thought their mates were less committed than they themselves were in their relationship. They asked 154 female students who were in relationships to list reasons why their partners might be either more or less committed to them. Those who scored higher on scales of narcissism found it twice as hard to think of reasons why their partners would be unhappy as opposed to reasons for their partners being happy with them. They felt pretty good about their relationship, however bad their partner felt. But this was largely because they couldn't imagine how anyone could be less than delighted by them.

Can people like this change? Perhaps only in Hollywood films where they get shot or have a brain hemorrhage and as they fight for life realize they're self-centered jerks and change into committed partners. But I wouldn't rely on that.

You're not a doormat for liking men with large egos; these men are popular. They are attractive for their enormous self-belief and outgoing personalities. But they don't want a real relationship, more a brief fling. Such people may not even realize the pain they cause, being so wrapped up in themselves. But while it's not your fault that you find these men attractive, you can still apply the brakes. Make sure you let relationships develop in their own time, through the initial attraction and "that's absolutely fascinating" to the reality of being a couple. Commitment isn't something that any normal person signs up for after the first few dates. Researchers from the University of Denver developed a scale to measure it, breaking commitment down into dedication ("I want to make our relationship work for both of us"), constraint ("why look for anyone else when I have you?"), and satisfaction. They found that couples could be extremely committed but not that satisfied with their relationships. So even if you have commitment, you still have to work on being happy together.

You are likely to meet someone right for a long-term relationship, and you'll know when it happens because he will act committed. So be more selective. Go for a man with a normal sized ego—the vast majority who can really love someone other than themselves.

Freudian Blip

I have read on more than one occasion that men are likely to choose romantic partners who remind them of their mothers. What if I in no way resemble his mother? Will the relationship last?

Are you sure you don't resemble your boyfriend's mother? It's oedipal to think of him wanting to go out with his mother but sweet to think he might want someone a bit like her. Researchers claim that both men and women are susceptible to sexual imprinting, defined as the sexual preference we have for individuals who look like our (opposite-sex) parent. The hypothesis is that by looking into someone's face as an infant you get a template by which to judge your future mate. But it's sex specific. Men don't want a lover who looks like their dad.

The adage that men should look at their wives' mothers to see how their wives will age is apparently out of date. Men should look at their own moms. This is shown by research in 2002 by Tamás Bereczkei, a Hungarian psychologist who compared over three hundred pictures of faces of family members with those of strangers. The people who acted as the judges in the study correctly matched wives to their husband's mothers more often than by chance (significantly so).

In a more recent study by Bereczkei, in the *Proceedings of the Royal Society B*, he identified more specifically the facial characteristics that people most look for in romantic partners (when they're unconsciously looking for a substitute for Mom or Dad). His team measured the facial proportions of 312 people from fifty-two Hungarian families. The matches between family members (which included a young man or woman, their long-term partner, and both sets of parents) were compared with those of randomly selected couples by independent judges. (It sounds more complicated than it is.) They found that young women resembled their partners' mothers in terms of how full their lips were, the width of their mouths, and the size of their jaws. Women went for men who had their dads' noses and a similar jaw-length to face-length ratio. This attraction has to be unconscious, unless your partner's taken a tape measure to the lower part of your face.

But the desire men seem to have for their mothers is not merely skin deep. Men want to have long-term relationships with women who are as smart as their mothers. A study by the sociologist Christine Whelan at the University of Iowa surveyed eight hundred men who earned salaries in the top 10 percent of their age group (they were in their twenties and thirties) and found that nearly 80 percent of those whose mothers had bachelor degrees had wives who were educated to a similar level.

However, even if you can't find anything in common with your partner's mother, there's no need to worry. There are many reasons why relationships last: how well you deal with conflict, how you share the housework, whether you have a laugh together, and what your sex life is like. I've yet to see a list that includes how much you resemble his mother.

Opportunity Knocks

Poached Partners

> I met this woman who's a friend of a friend, and I really like her. She's been seeing a guy and is about to move in with him. I'm twenty-eight, single, and everyone I meet these days is taken. Is it wrong to go after her? She can always say no.

Is it wrong? It's certainly rude—like sneezing into someone else's soup. Trying to steal someone else's partner is called "mate poaching" by relationship researchers, and for an underhanded, emotionally fraught, and morally iffy activity it is remarkably popular.

There's a lot of data on this. David Schmitt, from Bradley University in Illinois, led a study covering fifty-three countries that asked nearly seventeen thousand people if they'd ever tried to poach someone's partner or if someone had tried to poach them. The study, published in the *Personality and Social Psychology Bulletin*, shows that, on average, 60 percent of men and 40 percent of women have tried to poach someone. (In Asian and Middle Eastern countries the rates were lower than in the West. Nearly two-thirds of people said that someone had tried to poach them.) What are your chances of success with poaching? Around 50 percent of people who had a poaching attempt made on them went along with it. Men were more likely to do so than women, especially if it looked like a short-term poach—it's like having someone on loan.

There's no reason why poaching shouldn't result in a longer relationship; although usually it doesn't. In previous studies of college students (but replicated in older populations), Schmitt has shown that 15 percent of all current relationships started off as mate poaching.

There is an evolutionary element to this (which isn't an excuse because we all know better now). In times of war, famine, and pestilence lots of people lost their mates while they were relatively young. Most of the attractive people left were taken, so the widowed had to poach. In traditional hunter-gatherer cultures, according to Schmitt, mate poaching is common.

The methods that poachers use are simple but effective. One study refers to the poacher "slowly invading the target's social network." This means sidling up to his or her friends. Other methods include sowing seeds of dissatisfaction, such as sighing sympathetically and insincerely and saying, "I'm not sure your spouse really appreciates you." Overt flirting is a no-no, as would-be poachers risk getting a bloody nose from a jealous rival. During this underhanded activity you'll have to make sure your friends don't catch on to you. No one likes a poacher because no one wants someone to swipe *his or her own* partner.

The study also asked people about their personality types. You could take an educated guess; poachers score highly on being unconscientious, outgoing, selfish, unempathic, and talkative. They major in self-disclosure, especially about sex. Those who are successfully poached also score more highly on being outgoing and liking to talk about sex. The talking is clearly a prelude to having it. As you might expect, attractive, self-confident people are better at poaching.

Although no one likes poaching, there's a lot of it going on. Maybe if the woman you are trying to poach says yes, you deserve each other. The studies showed that the poacher and the poached both had high scores for unfaithfulness.

Office Romance

I've been friends with a new guy at work for a few months. I've always thought he was gorgeous, and now he's said he's very attracted to me. I'd really like to start seeing him—we are both nearly thirty—but we work in the same department and I like my job too. Is it a mistake to have a relationship with someone you work with?

He's not your boss—which is good. But you get points deducted for working in the same department. There's a risk of competition between you, and being an item within a team can be claustrophobic. You are sensible, if not sufficiently blinded by love, to see the potential for disaster. Grim indeed to sit in meetings with a still-steaming ex. But let's be practical; you have to meet Mr. Right or Wrong somewhere. Around four out of ten people in the United States admit to having had workplace romances, according to a survey by

Harris Interactive of 1,588 employees for the recruitment firm Spherion Corporation. This and other surveys show that around six out of ten of us have at least one long-term relationship (including marriage) with people we meet at work.

You're more likely to meet your future mate at work than pretty much anywhere else. It's partly an exposure thing—in terms of time and proximity. A survey in *Psychology Today* says that one-third of work romances are between people in the same or adjoining offices. Apparently we're too lazy to check out the talent downstairs.

Your workplace has already done the screening work of a dating service—combining people who share ambitions and interests and often cultural values. You may learn more about someone by working with them than going out on any number of dates. Working closely together builds familiarity, intimacy, and trust. These don't sound sexy, but strangely they are. Work itself can be arousing—all those deadlines and anxiety, all those late-into-the-evening sessions and bonding in a bar afterward. And who better to understand the pressure of your work than the person sitting at the desk behind you?

Dr. Lisa Mainiero, a professor of management at the Fairfield University School of Management in Connecticut, surveyed over one hundred female executives to determine the characteristics of those office romances that worked. Those most likely to succeed are between peers from different departments. Couples should agree how they'll behave at work (no kissing, fighting, or blabbing about their relationship) and what they will do if they split up (be professional). Remember, the odds are that most office romances will end, so at least try to think things through. While two-thirds of office romances start in secret, Mainiero's research shows that coworkers invariably figure out what's going on, and that it's the serious relationships that quickly go public. Most people will be happy

36

You Can Count on Cupid

for you—everyone loves a lover. But around one-third of office romances are between people already in other relationships, and these really aren't popular at all.

So as long as he isn't too distracting and you don't tell your colleagues at work about either your fights or your unbelievable sex, you should be fine. Ideally he'd get a job in another department. Not too far away, though, or he might get interested in someone else.

One Night Only

> I met this guy at a friend's wedding four weeks ago, and we had a fantastic time dancing and drinking together. We had sex that night, and although the next morning he said he'd call me, he hasn't. I hadn't meant it to be a one-night stand. Do you think the fact we had sex so quickly has put him off?

You could always call him and ask. Sex on the first date doesn't preclude a lifetime of happiness together. But if you're asking whether it's a good idea to have sex on the first date, the answer is no. Unless there are bombs falling and you don't think there will be a tomorrow.

This hard-line approach is for self-preservation, because sex on the first date is usually influenced by one of the three *D*'s: drink, drugs, or desperation. Sex is not a fast track to cementing a relationship, and unless you have a PhD in sexual pleasuring you won't increase your desirability as a partner by having sex with someone you've known for only a few hours. The encounter is rarely satisfying sexually and can be embarrassing afterward.

A one-night stand has the expectation that the relationship

will end before noon the next day. Such sex without strings has to be okay if you both agreed to it—but people don't have that chat first. Hence the ambiguity the morning after. An *Observer* poll carried out by Independent Communications and Marketing (ICM) of one thousand Britons in 2008 found that more than half had had a one-night stand, but other surveys range from 10 to 50 percent. If there's a perception that everyone is having sex with each other immediately, the reality is different. A Market and Opinion Research International (MORI) poll of 1,790 adults showed most waited one to three weeks before having sex with their current partner. According to the same poll, only one in ten men and 3 percent of women had sex on the first date. An ABC News *Primetime Live* survey of 1,501 American adults found that 29 percent had had sex on their first date.

Would you have regretted not having sex with him? A study from Arizona State University on lifetime regrets of 120 men and women showed that vastly more men than women regretted not "trying harder to sleep with" someone. Women had an even mixture of regrets about the people they had and hadn't had sex with. This may be because some women, you included, consider sex to be more than a recreational activity.

That's not to say it can't be a recreational activity, but public opinion is still against the idea. In a recent study by Dr. Sharon Hinchliff of Sheffield University in England, forty-six British women between the ages of twenty and eighty-three were asked their opinion on casual sex. Ninety percent thought casual sex was wrong and done out of neediness rather than sexual liberation. Some younger women were harsher than older ones, and only 10 percent of all the women admitted to having had one-night stands themselves. Those who had had one disapproved as much as those who hadn't. Men's attitudes are likely to be less harsh. Another study of public opinion comes from a questionnaire survey from Texas Tech University in the journal *Personal Relationships*. This study, of 148 men and 148 women, found that while women and men thought less of people who had sex on a first date, they thought equally badly of men and women. Which has to be progress of sorts.

So there still seems to be a stigma about the one-night stand that *Sex and the City* hasn't dispelled. In fact, among single women over forty, only 2 percent approved of sex on the first date according to an AARP survey of 1,407 men and 2,094 women. However, none of these statistics mean your guy should think any less of you. After all, he was there too.

Tall Story

> I am short (five foot one) and my husband is six foot one. I have never been attracted to small men, though that would be a more normal-looking couple. Someone told me it's because short women need tall men to have children of average size. Is this why I fell for him?

I'm sure there's more to your husband than his height, but studies show that generally women prefer taller men and that men prefer smaller women. In 2000 the UK's National Child Development Study analyzed data from ten thousand people born in a single week in March 1958. The taller the men were (above the average of five foot ten), the more likely they were to be married with children. Women were most likely to be married and have children if they were between four foot nine and five foot one (the average is around five foot four). The study's authors are not sure why men prefer short women, but in evolutionary terms tall women are seen as less fertile because they tend to reach puberty later than shorter women. However, there's no evidence that taller women conceive less quickly or less often than shorter women today.

Many studies show that women find taller men more attractive: tall, dark, and handsome men to be precise. They correlate height with health, wealth, and status, which is pretty accurate. Unfortunately for shorter men, research does show a basic link between social deprivation and height. A study of 3,200 Polish men found unmarried and childless men were an inch shorter than those who were married with children. Women were found actively to select taller men, although it wasn't height that won them over but the desirable qualities they inferred from it. And women are not alone in believing taller men are better. Studies show the belief that taller is better for men is a genuine, widespread phenomenon; there's evidence that taller men are more likely to be selected for jobs, chosen for promotion, and if they're politicians, voted for by the electorate.

Surely there's some evidence that we're not as shallow as this suggests? Studies of singles ads show that 80 percent of women who requested meeting men of a certain height wanted someone over six feet tall, and almost all of them wanted a man who was at least four inches taller than they were. However, once on dates common sense trumps evolution, and they're more likely to rate other factors such as personality and intelligence as just as important as height.

Genetic studies suggest a link between the heights of mother and son and of father and daughter. The authors of the UK National Child Development Study say that taller fathers have taller daughters. In your case this would bring any daughter you had up to an average height. Even so, it's less the height adjustment for your kids that made you marry him and more what you thought being tall represented. Let's hope he delivers on both counts.

Dumb Choice

I'm a thirty-year-old single woman, and I have no trouble finding dates. However, they rarely progress beyond the first date, and I get the feeling I am intimidating men. A friend recommended I act "stupid" on dates because men don't like women who appear to be more intelligent, confident, and attractive than them. Is my friend right?

As a strategy, "acting stupid" has limitations. When do you plan to reveal the real you? Evolutionary psychologists say that men want women who are great at childbearing (so men should look at teeth and muscle tone) and that women like men with fat wallets (so check the inside pocket). Can it be that we haven't moved with the times at all? A survey published in *Sex Roles* of 199 people in Amsterdam showed only a minority interest in the intelligence of a future mate. Physical attractiveness as well as being honest, reliable, and fun to be with came out on top for both sexes. Men cared more about looks than women. And there are many studies that replicate these findings. However, women may overestimate the extent to which men are intimidated by intelligent women. A Match.com survey found that while most men said they'd be happy to marry a career-minded woman (who one assumes would be intelligent), most women thought it would put men off.

Anecdotally, men say they want women who are almost as smart as them (the "almost" is of critical importance). There are, however, no anecdotes suggesting men want someone less attractive. But how attractive is a woman with a high IQ?

A study led by Michelle Taylor from the University of Edinburgh in Scotland and published in the journal *Personality and Individual Differences* compared the IQ tests of nine hundred people taken at age eleven with their marriageable status forty years later. For every sixteen-point rise in IQ, women were 40 percent less likely to be married. When this finding was reported in the media, women shuddered. But it could mean that women know marriage benefits men more than women and decide not to get married. It's also worth noting that the study looked at men and women who were born in 1921 and whose attitudes are likely to be rather different than those of younger men and women. Still, we can't rule out that smart women do intimidate men, although more recent research suggests such men are in the minority. A study conducted by Megan M. Sweeny, a sociologist at the University of California, Los Angeles, shows that an increase of $10,000 in earning boosts the likelihood of a woman marrying within a year by 7 percent. Heather Boushey, an economist at the Center for Economic and Policy Research in Washington, D.C., found that of women between the ages of thirty and forty-four who earn more than $100,000 a year, 88 percent are married, compared with 82 percent of other women of the same age group.

If marriage prospects are similar, what about the likelihood of divorce? It used to be thought that women who were college graduates were more likely to divorce, perhaps because they were more likely to be financially independent afterward. But more recent research, including a study from the University of Maryland looking at sixteen thousand marriages between 1990 and 1994, shows that where a wife had a college education the chances of divorce in the first ten years were

16.5 percent compared with 38 percent when the wife did not have further education.

Being too opinionated, not listening, and seeming uninterested in your date will put men off. Being overconfident is also unattractive. Dates may make you anxious and more intimidating than you either realize or mean to be. These behaviors are more likely to scare men off than your intelligence. Relax and play nice rather than dumb.

First Mover

> I really like this guy who is the friend of a friend of mine. I've met him a few times. We see each other at parties and talk to each other, but nothing has ever come of it. I know he is single, so if he liked me he would have done something about it by now. So shall I forget about dating him or try to find out if he is interested?

It should be easy to know if someone is interested in you, but it isn't. All this platonic interaction makes for a blurring of boundaries between friendships and romantic relationships. It's possible to go on a date without knowing it. But even in times of strict dating convention there were still ambiguities. Jane Austen's novels often revolve around questions of "Does (insert name of uptight romantic hero) fancy me or not?"

It's highly possible for people to misconstrue romantic intentions, and conventions are meant to help. Going up to someone in a bar and asking them if they'd like a drink is a recognized sign of interest. Other more subtle ones, such as a man leaning toward you, engaging you in exclusive conversation, and locking eyes with you are harder to gauge. He may just be strange or intense. Studies show an overlap between many of the qualities people look for in their friends and those that they want in potential romantic partners. They may not be sure themselves which way the connection will go until they know each other better. Conversely, some people (and they may be the happier ones) construe more interest from people they meet than actually exists.

You don't know if your guy is interested or not. Men are still expected to make the first move, but not all of them do it all of the time, and he may think you won't be interested. Maybe he can't tell that you like him more than anyone else in your group of friends because you haven't given him any reason to hope. No one likes rejection, and it's awkward to ask someone out and see the horror in his or her face. Take a sweet academic study in the *Journal of Social and Personal Relationships* that involved 522 people and is called "Who's Going to Make the First Move? Pluralistic Ignorance as an Impediment to Relationship Formation." "Pluralistic ignorance" refers to how people see someone behaving like them (i.e., not asking them out) but infer they're doing so for different reasons. So neither of you is making a move, but although you're attracted to him, you assume he's not interested. This research looked at previous smaller studies and hypothetical scenarios, but the finding that self-protection can override romantic imperative seems fairly obvious, though it points to a rather feeble way to live your life.

Go-betweens like your friend can help (tell your friend you're interested), and you can try to assess (with others) whether he likes you. Try flirting with someone standing next to him and see if he flinches. Actually, don't. A far better idea is to be brave and ask him out for a drink. There's some evidence that it will be the lesser of two evils. Most people can get over rejection, especially from someone they don't know that well, whereas a study from Cornell University of what people regret most found that one of the most common regrets people had in their lives was missing a romantic opportunity.

Wish You Were Here

> I'm going on vacation with friends, and I'm hoping to meet someone as I've been single for a while. But when I've had holiday romances in the past, they've been disastrous. Why does this happen—are holiday romances doomed?

Holiday romances are not known for their longevity. What can it be about sun, bare flesh, a gallon of something you'd never drink at home, and a week of sleeping in late that promotes romance or, to be more cynical, casual sex? You need to be cautious about trying to start a long-term relationship on vacation, because the normal rules of engagement are suspended.

If you meet someone at home, maybe you'll start off by seeing each other a few times over the first couple of weeks. On vacation you can see each other all day, every day. You may not be able to avoid it. Suddenly this is the most intense relationship you've ever had, and, what's more, it's so easy—you're both so open (and often so drunk) and so passionate. And it's so unrealistic. Real life is more mundane. There's no context to refer to when you see someone in swimwear at the pool bar.

Surveys by interested parties such as condom manufacturers, travel companies, and doctors specializing in sexually transmitted diseases (was there really no room to pack the condoms?) show that between one-fifth and one-half of the adults in the United States and Great Britain had a holiday romance. Who knows how many people find the man or woman of their dreams (or even want to)? A Sky Travel survey of 2,000 people found only one in ten holiday romances lasted longer than a week, but an Ipsos/MORI poll of 505 people put it closer to half, and an *Observer* (London) poll found that 20 percent became long-term relationships. But what would be the percentages for those who read the *Observer* but also use Sky Travel services? That's hard to quantify.

In the United Kingdom, a research paper in the journal *Sexually Transmitted Infections* said that one in five British people (based on the study of twelve thousand adults between the ages of sixteen and forty-four) had had sex with a new partner while abroad. Since sexual survey statistics in the United States are usually close to those in the United Kingdom, the rates may be fairly similar. Some people have no intention of embarking on a serious relationship. Researchers from St. George's Hospital in London asked 150 people in the airport departure hall at the Spanish island of Tenerife about sex on their holiday. Surprisingly, they weren't told to get lost, and they found that 48 out of 136 people had had sex with someone other than their partner (but then the travel agents had offered champagne to the first new couple to have sex).

Sometimes the holiday romance is taken more seriously by one person than the other. In a study that asked thirty-five women about their holiday encounters, Michelle Thomas from Cardiff University in Wales found that although women often felt incredibly close to their new partner while on vacation, their trust was sometimes misplaced. It was not uncommon, for example, for men not to mention their girlfriend at home until after they'd had sex. Thomas warns that time becomes compressed on vacations and caution is thrown to the wind.

Why you shouldn't follow suit is that you want this to be for real. Many holiday romances are casual because people want them to fade before their tan does. Most people have holiday romances with people from their own country—it's more convenient. There are people who fall in love with locals and never go home, but probably not many. No one can help you with the choosing; but the bars of Tenerife, Acapulco, and Phuket, Thailand, are not full of people looking for commitment. If you do meet someone, take it steady, and make it clear that you are looking for a relationship longer than a week. Don't spend all your time with this individual; you're holidaying with friends. Don't dilute your judgment with too much alcohol, and don't intensify the relationship. Follow a more "at home" trajectory. If you do make it home, do the dating thing rather than assume you've been catapulted into the status of established couple. And don't take too many photos—it's tempting fate.

Ex or Hex?

> One of my best friends broke up with her boyfriend four months ago. I always thought he was gorgeous, and when I saw him recently we talked all evening and had a goodnight kiss. He said he wanted to see me again. Their split was mutual. Shall I ask my friend if it's okay to see him, or forget about him?

"All's fair in love and war" is one way of looking at things; another is "Thou shalt not date your friend's ex." Find out your friend's view before you proceed, or risk losing her forever. It's unsettling to think of a friend sleeping with your ex, however mutual the split was or however average the sex. These sorts of relationships are referred to as a form of recycling (celebrities are forever going out with friends' exes) or even by the horrible term "sloppy seconds." There's an implication that the subsequent partner is second best. Yet the likelihood of being attracted to a friend's partner is fairly high. Friends are usually like us in terms of their age, education, what they earn, and how attractive they are, and people tend to be attracted to people who are similar to them. So you're more likely to be similar to your friend's partner than a stranger in a club. You'll also know the partner better, having hung out with this person socially and heard intimate details from your friend. It's good manners to ignore any attraction, but there's an inevitable sexual rivalry between friends when it comes to finding lovers.

Studies (mostly of undergraduates, who may be more susceptible to this) show that nearly one in five men and 29 percent of women have flirted with a friend's partner and that over half have competed with a friend to attract a potential partner. In a study of young people carried out by researchers at the University of Texas at Austin, forty-eight men and sixty-nine women were asked to rank the costs and benefits of their (same-sex) friends. Out of ten costs, the highest ranking was, sadly, being treated cruelly by a friend; stealing boyfriends or girlfriends ranked fifth. Perhaps the two costs are related.

In another study, of 406 college students from universities in the South and Southwest of the United States and published in *Personal Relationships*, 67 percent of people said they were the victim of "intrasexual rivalry" from a friend, although they *may* have used different words to describe it.

This is not to say you have poached your friend's ex yet, but if stealing a boyfriend is disloyalty as an art form, dating one even after the relationship is over is not going to delight your friend. Some friends and even some exes will take a "waste not, want not" view. Your friend may, however, wonder if you always lusted after her ex, making the conversations you may have had about the relationship dishonest and self-interested on your part.

I could find no research on whether these relationships last. You're likely to be similar (that's good), but your friends may not like it (that's bad). Out of courtesy, ask your friend if it's okay, but "It's absolutely fine" is unlikely to mean that. Expect your friendship to change (not for the better), and so only start a romance if you think it will be worth it. And remember, your friend won't want to hear the intimate details.

Unsettling Thoughts

> After a two-year failed relationship, I decided to move abroad to pursue my artistic ambitions. I wanted to enjoy "exploring" men and relationships, but now I find I am already involved with someone I care for but who has no goals or ambitions. I feel disappointed in him and am dating other men—and have told him. If I really loved him, would I do this? At forty-one should I stop making excuses for not being in a stable relationship and settle down?

In your question you're really asking yourself what to do. Which is a relief because you're the person in the best position to know.

Everyone settles for someone to some degree. Otherwise we'd all have rich, beautiful, exciting, yet trustworthy mates—the type the research says we want. Some would argue it's better to be single than settle for less than ideal, but that depends on how realistic you are. When you ask people more specifically about long-term relationships, they say they want romantic partners who are faithful and good companions—which sounds like a dog, until you get to the third requirement: good sex. These characteristics scored highest in an Australian survey of 1,200 people (the Relationships Indicators Survey) and a survey of 2,020 Americans by the Pew Research Center. A partner's standing in life wasn't mentioned as a choice.

The importance of compatibility, however, was raised by one in ten of the Australian survey and is as high in other surveys. Ambitious people like you might struggle to commit to someone who seems "goalless." If he disappoints you now, the natural history of relationships suggests he won't delight you later.

If you want to settle, there's good evidence for what you should look for. The research suggests that the adage "birds of a feather flock together" is more accurate than "opposites attract." True.com, an evidence-based online compatibility test developed in the United States, looks at 616 characteristics. Some key things that matter are how well you talk to each other (it's good if you open up and don't mind making yourself vulnerable), how you get over arguments (negotiate and don't sulk), and how happy you are with your sex life. If you meet someone who is conscientious, deals well with stress, is sensible with money, and has good parenting skills, you won't be settling but winning the lottery. But you do need to be compatible in terms of how adventurous you are, your ambitions, and your sociability. Differences in any of these areas can be remarkably disruptive for couples.

The average age for marrying has gone up in the developed world in the past few decades from twenty-seven and a half for men and twenty-five and a half for women to nearly thirty-two for men and twenty-nine and a half for women in 2001. There's also some evidence that settling later is better, so if you don't want children, don't rush. You may, however, have heard of the demographic study *Marriage Patterns in the United States*, which was reported in 1986 in *Newsweek* as finding that "a single forty-year-old woman has a better chance of being killed by a terrorist than getting married (a 2.6 percent chance)." It wasn't true; other researchers were quick to recalculate the chance of getting married as up to 23 percent, and others have since said it's even higher. I'd suggest you explore what you want first before you explore any other men.

Rebound to Fail?

> I've met this guy whom I really like, but four months ago he came out of a long-term relationship (he says it was a mutual decision). I'm worried that he'll use me as a "transitional" person to get over his relationship and then move on. How can I tell if his feelings for me are real or if he's just on the rebound?

You're worried about being used and dumped, which can happen in any relationship. But there's something about a rebounding lover that strikes fear into any heart that's still beating. Dr. Gilda Carle, author of *Don't Bet on the Prince: How to Have the Man You Want by Betting on Yourself*, is unsurprisingly (given her book's title) not a fan of rebound relationships. She warns not to get involved with anyone less than nine months after they've come out of a serious relationship. The perceived wisdom is that rebounders need to grieve and work out why their last relationship unraveled. This assumes people learn from their previous relationships rather than just go out with their pals for a few drinks. Another way of looking at things is expressed in the old saying, "The best way to get over a man is to get under the next one." The Web site rebound-relationships.com says that rebound relationships can be unrealistically fast paced, with the rebounder moving on to a "proper relationship" quite quickly. Tips for spotting a rebounder include persistent sniveling over an ex, an unrealistically speedy attachment to you (proposing can be an extreme variant), and neediness or bitterness toward the opposite sex.

Along with this largely anecdotal evidence comes some research from Nicholas H. Wolfinger, a demographer at the University of Utah. His study of 1,171 adults in the National Survey of Families and Households found that as far as marriage or living together (and then going on to marry) was concerned, there was no rebound effect. Couples who rushed into second marriages were no more likely to split up than those who waited longer. Second marriages are more likely to end than first ones, but how quickly people rush into them doesn't seem to affect their longevity. Wolfinger says he couldn't look at dating because the data hasn't been collected. He also told me that as a demographer he's agnostic about what's in people's heads—he does the counting, not the psychoanalysis.

In Britain, John Ermisch of the Institute for Social and Economic Research found that one-half of people who leave a cohabiting relationship and 30 percent of divorced people find new partners within two years. The study doesn't say much about emotional recovery, but psychologist Judith Wallerstein's research estimated that it took women three years to feel stable after a divorce, while men were feeling much better after an average of two years. However, her study was carried out in the 1980s, and as divorce has become more common, recovery may be quicker. Wolfinger believes that people vary in how quickly they recover from divorce. Most of the upheaval, such as moving, takes place in the first year after splitting up, and some people need to feel settled before they can start dating again.

Common sense suggests you take things at a normal, non-rebound pace; don't expect him to feel nothing for his ex, but it's reasonable that he shouldn't see her. You may need to be supportive but maintain some distance and an independent social life. If he's got any sense, he'll reassure you that it's you he wants to be with.

3

After the First Few Dates

Can't Hurry Love

> I'm thirty-seven and have been seeing a man who is
> nothing like my previous boyfriends. He is loving,
> thoughtful, and clever. Usually I go for "action" men
> and lust. This relationship didn't start like that. I en-
> joy having sex with him and think I love him. But for
> a long-term relationship, shouldn't I be in love with
> him? Can I make myself fall in love with him?

For long-term relationships the script usually requires that
you should be *in* love. But psychology researchers and anyone
with half a brain can work out that there are two types of love
in relationships. The first is the romantic type that develops
rapidly and becomes an obsession. You're either with them or
thinking about being with them, all of the time. Passion is a pre-
requisite, and obsession and jealousy are frequent side effects.

Then there's companionate (friendship-type) love that grows strongly with time and is driven by coming to know someone deeply—often in ways that nobody else knows (or would want to know). Guess which one's the better bedrock for an enduring relationship?

As president of the International Association for Relationship Research, Dr. Robert Milardo knows quite a bit about love. He believes that falling in love is an intentional phenomenon, however magical it feels. You couldn't fall in love with just anyone; you have to find the person attractive and share some values—and you have to want to do it. We all focus, albeit unconsciously, on the aspects we find most attractive in a person, even as we're falling.

You're quite clear that it's been about lust before, and you like the fact this man offers more. What worries you is that he didn't offer up the lust first. Each year Milardo asks his twenty-eight students in relationships studies whether it's best to start off with romantic or friendship-type love in a relationship. In 2007 nearly all of them said having friendship first gave the relationship a more solid basis. A broader survey of over two hundred engaged American men and women in their twenties found that three-quarters rejected the definition of their relationship as being "head over heels in love."

I'm afraid there are no meaningful statistics to help you. There are no studies on falling in love with someone because you want to. No one would sign up for a randomized controlled trial that assigned you a lover on the throw of a coin. All the studies can tell you is that it's companionate and not passionate love that makes for intimate and sound relationships. They're not mutually exclusive, and either can come first. Everyone knows couples who started off as friends and then fell in love.

Statistics aside, academics can't even agree on what love

is—an emotion or, as one research paper put it, "a goal-oriented motivational state." Arguments rage over whether there is a facial expression for love (as there is for joy or sorrow). Surveys of ordinary folk show they do rate love as an emotion; in particular, they say it makes them happy to think about the person they love. Being in love generally includes sexual desire (you like having sex with him) and feeling good about yourself.

There are studies of arranged marriages, but they wouldn't help you—the religious and cultural differences make the results inapplicable. After all, you are able to choose. I suggest you choose someone you want to do the business of loving and living with.

Friendly Fire

> My friends don't like my boyfriend. Some knew him from college, where he had a reputation for being unfaithful to his girlfriends, but that was three years ago. They make excuses about why they can't meet us and keep asking me why I'm with him. I don't feel we can go out with my friends as they seem so hostile. What should I do?

Any man who has been unfaithful to girlfriends (I note the plural) will not score highly with your friends. For while friends might get jealous when you start a relationship (worrying you'll have less time for them), they mostly want you to be happy. They either fear he won't make you happy or dislike him for other reasons. In your case it's more obvious than in most why they might dislike him.

No relationship is an island; it's surrounded by friends and

55

family, all of whom have something to say about it. Unfortunately, most research focuses on how couples develop their relationships in isolation, rather than seeing how their social network affects them. A 1972 study in the *Journal of Personality and Social Psychology* discovered "a Romeo and Juliet effect" (a term applied to many relationship issues by researchers), where parents who disapproved and interfered with the relationship made it stronger. Other studies have not replicated these historical findings and instead show that it is parental approval that nourishes relationships. How conventional we've become.

This is shown in a more recent study of 101 dating couples conducted at the University of Illinois. If you are not twenty and attending a university in the Midwest, be cautious in applying the results to your own life; but as you'll see, the conclusions are more commonsensical than wildly radical. The study found that both men and women felt happier and were more committed to each other when their friends approved of their relationship. When friends tell a couple they're a good match and how much they enjoy going out with them, that couple starts believing they really are a couple. What's more, they'll think they make a good couple. And when friends say, "He's a great guy really, he didn't mean to throw up on you," it makes you less likely to dump him. Friends (women in particular) can either support or trash relationships by adding information into the mix when they're analyzing the relationship. Which they do continuously. When a couple stays together for a while, their groups of friends start to overlap and this strengthens the relationship. (However, in this study, where couples were young, many of the relationships didn't last long anyway.)

So if you're happy in your relationship and think your boyfriend is a reformed character, you need to raise the issue with your friends and, if need be, stand up for him. Are they being overprotective because of rumors, or do they dislike him for who he is now? Do they think he's boring? Do they think he treats you badly? (You might want to look at that too.) You may have to reconcile yourself to seeing your friends without him. But don't alienate your friends, because if he does turn out to be a philandering scumbag you'll really want them around.

Round the Bend

> My girlfriend is a terrible driver, and every time we go on trips together we have huge arguments that can end up with her pulling over and stopping. When I drive, she'll criticize my driving too. Do most couples argue in the car? Why do they do this, and how can we stop?

Cars are small, confined spaces, which make them ideal to fight in. Asking why couples argue in a car is like asking why childbirth is painful. It's part of the human condition. Arguments accelerate in a car faster than you can go from zero to thirty miles per hour, and unless you pull over there's no escape.

A 2007 ICM Research poll of 2,071 drivers over eighteen years of age found that one in ten (really so few?) will be arguing with their partner within fifteen minutes of starting their car journey. About 40 percent of the arguments are caused by men criticizing their partners' driving. Just over one in ten are caused by men taking control of the car stereo. (After a bitter radio custody battle my partner once pulled off the volume knob; oh, how we laughed.) But this antipathy from men is not limited to who's in the car with them; they'll argue with anyone on the road. The survey also found that while almost all women had lost their temper while driving, it was overwhelmingly with male drivers.

Since men and women are essentially arguing over who's the best driver, what does the research show? As an extreme measure you could look at fatality rates. Put grimly, who kills the most people on the road? The answer is clear-cut. The Fatality Analysis Reporting System in Washington, D.C., compared deaths in motor crashes between 1996 and 2006 and found they were higher for men than women in all age groups (even though the number of men in the population was the same or lower in each age group). The Traffic STATS site at the Transportation Research Board in Washington puts an actual percentage on it—men are 77 percent more likely to die in car crashes than women. Other studies suggest why this might be the case: men take more risks. Researchers at Wright State University in Ohio have shown that men drivers who die in car crashes are more likely than women drivers to have driven while drunk, driven at night, and had previous traffic convictions and crashes. Now you could argue that this doesn't mean women are better drivers. But personally I wouldn't—and nor would some car insurers.

Interestingly, in 2001 the United Kingdom's Advertising Standards Authority ruled that an insurance company could advertise cheaper car insurance for women because they "are better drivers" (the measure being involvement in fewer accidents). The Social Issues Research Centre (SIRC) published a report on sex differences in driving, citing evidence from the World Health Organization that men (especially those under twenty-five) are more aggressive drivers, more likely to speed, not wear seat belts, and crash. Poor men; the SIRC says they carry a larger "interpersonal bubble," and when someone goes near it they can get road rage. A classic accident for men is taking a turn too quickly after having been cut off by another driver.

Women, however, are more likely to be involved in more minor accidents, what could be passed off as "errors of judgment." Their accidents are caused by carelessly pulling out of intersections or by misjudging the proximity of the car that's ahead of or behind them. But as Professor Frank McKenna of the University of Reading in England once told a transport conference, "Precious few people die parking." Other research, from Johns Hopkins University, argues that women drive less than men and that this may account for their having an overall lower rate of crashes.

At least disputes about map reading can now be solved by satellite navigation. Research shows that most arguments are best resolved by humor and compromise rather than sulking. You can stop arguing by not getting in the same car. Criticizing your partner's driving is going to cause a fight, so you'll have to exercise self-control and stop doing it. But if you must drive together, the American Automobile Association warns that distracting the driver causes up to half of accidents. However, you're more likely to crash looking at scenery or nodding off, so arguing may not be so bad after all.

Split the Difference?

About two years ago I found new happiness with a lovely divorced man with two teenagers. While acknowledging the value of the connection, he suddenly withdrew, saying he couldn't commit and admitting cowardice, while insisting he is happy as a bachelor. It seems so sad—I truly have yet to meet a nicer man. Is he just afraid, or is this a polite way of

breaking it off after a few months of mutual enjoy-
ment?

If he says he is breaking it off because he can't commit and is
a coward, you'll have to believe him. The alternative is to ac-
cuse him of lying to save your feelings and insist that he tell
you he doesn't like you enough (even if it's not true). Either
way, it's over, and his reason sounds sufficiently honest to be
genuine. If there's anything left to understand, it's probably
that some people don't want to commit to close relationships
after they've gotten divorced. Many studies show that while
women experience more stress during a divorce, men have it
later and for longer and are more likely to smoke, drink, throw
themselves into work, and engage in "frantic sexual activity,"
as one study so nicely puts it, in attempts to get over it. Men
often mourn the loss of their children and home more than
their wives. However, the research isn't consistent, with some
studies showing little difference in how men and women cope
with divorce. Having friends and family to talk to is helpful for
both sexes as long as they don't tell you where you went
wrong.

Your nice man may have had such a bad experience of
marriage that he's become cynical and less willing to commit.
Maybe he never had the support he needed to cope with his
divorce. Perhaps he also knows that bringing children (especially teenagers) into any new relationship increases the chances
of the relationship ending with everyone in tears. Maybe he understands the responsibilities and risks of commitment and
doesn't want them—even with someone he enjoyed being with
as much as you.

Of course, many divorced people do have further committed relationships. A study by the Institute of Social and
Economic Research using data from the British Household

Panel Survey found that 43 percent of divorced people will have another partner within five years, a lower percentage than that for people who split up after living together. This is partly because people who are living together are on average younger. Men are twice as likely to remarry as women.

But these statistics are population-based—they can't tell you anything about your man. A study of 208 divorced people published in the *Journal of Marriage and Family* showed that people found it harder to get over a divorce if they were older and hadn't wanted one and did better if they had a new relationship. You should stop torturing yourself over what he really meant and accept what he is saying; he is a nice man, you had a good time, but he prefers being single. You, however, would prefer not to be single, so you need to keep looking. Don't get hung up on his being "the one," because—without wishing to sound unromantic (or confusing)—there's more than one right one for everyone.

Romeo and Juliet

> I'm in a relationship with a girl I knew from college. We have mutual friends and kept it secret in case it didn't work out. Now that we're more open about our relationship, she's rapidly lost interest in me. Would this have happened if we'd still kept our relationship secret, or does it show she wasn't really interested?

The trouble with secret relationships is that it's hard to know how interested either of you really is. Secret relationships feel hot because the secrecy increases the excitement. They are the stuff of plays (*Romeo and Juliet*). But do they make people happy? They don't in plays, where lovers end up drinking poison, nor in real life, because secrecy gets in the way of building a commitment. People sometimes hide relationships (as they do early pregnancies) until they think they're viable. Workplace romances, affairs with married people, inter-religious or gay relationships may be hidden for longer out of fear that colleagues, family, or friends may disapprove. The rationale that a couple will be less embarrassed if it doesn't work out if no one knew about it in the first place is somewhat misguided. Once a secret relationship is over, everyone knows.

The corrosive (rather than enhancing) effect of secrecy (you might think shared secrets bring people closer) is shown in a study from the University of Georgia published in *Personal Relationships*. Researchers asked 201 women and thirty-nine men between the ages of sixteen and thirty-nine who were in relationships if they were keeping them secret, and if so, how much pressure that created. They also asked them how upset they'd be if the relationship ended. Of the thirty-five who had secret relationships, most said they'd be less upset. Also, they were more likely to feel their relationship was a burden.

The same research team conducted a further study of forty-six people in secret relationships and found that, compared to people in public relationships, they were less satisfied with their romantic partners and rated their relationships as poorer. After the initial excitement, the quality of secret relationships falls quickly because it's too much like hard work. Most people in secret relationships get fed up with lying to friends about why they're not around some weekends and with reassuring their family that being single is great. There's also the problem of secrecy being a barrier to couples getting close; in a secret relationship you can't talk to other people about how you feel and get support for the relationship. You can't even cuddle each other in public. By not going public you can't acknowledge to the world that the other person is special to you. Since relationships are about being special to someone else, this means that secret relationships have a serious design flaw.

Secrecy may be intense, but it denies a couple the fun of early relationships and the opportunity to get to know each other. It can be hard to know what's more interesting, the person or the secrecy. Going public is often a turning point: it's not unusual to find that once the secrecy's gone there isn't much left.

Poles Apart

> Do opposites attract? My girlfriend loves traveling and opera and has political leanings to the right. Traveling is okay, but I hate opera and have always been politically to the left. We get along really well, but will these differences matter in the long term?

Only when you're dealing with magnetic poles do opposites attract. Relationship research would say it's conclusively proven that like attracts like. The term "assortative mating" refers to the idea that there's a systematic pattern in how people choose mates (and mostly they seem to pick people like themselves). In measuring this phenomenon, most research has rated the characteristics of one partner against the other's. It has found that couples usually share religious and political beliefs and are about the same age. They are fairly similar in their education, intelligence, and what they think matters in life. Most people go for someone as good-looking or plain as they are (excluding rich people who most people seem to find gorgeous). Part of the explanation for who we choose lies in who we meet. At work, at your gym, and at a friend's party, you'll meet people quite like you.

You may, however, also be familiar with the saying "love is blind," suggesting you can fall for anyone, should you get the chance to meet them. But psychologists argue it's temporary; after three months you can see again, and usually the love fades. There's a strong drive to see similarities in someone you're attracted to even when they don't exist. A small, not very scientific study conducted at the University of Maine in the 1980s asked sixty men to rank on a questionnaire how similar a woman was to them. Those that found her attractive were nearly twice as likely to find her remarkably similar to themselves as those who didn't. Another study by researchers at the University of Notre Dame and published in *Personal Relationships* asked 301 college students who were in relationships how similar they were to their other half. (People were recruited as couples into the study and their mean age was around twenty.) The researchers asked each half of the couples about their ability to be emotionally close to others, how secure they felt, and how much they felt their significant other understood them. The study showed that couples who felt the closest to each other were most likely to think their partner was just like them—even when they scored quite differently on the psychological tests.

If you differ in some areas, even religion, you may still have a great relationship. Why your differences may not matter may come down to your personalities. A *Journal of Personality and Social Psychology* study at Iowa University of 291 newlywed couples who had dated for three and a half years found that in a committed relationship it was similarities in personalities (such as how open or caring someone is) that kept couples happy and helped them negotiate their differences, for example, what music they preferred to have on in the car. Usually couples seem to hook up on the basis of skin-deep similarities and wait to see if the relationship works out. You, on the other hand, may have chosen more wisely, and it's the similarities in your personalities that will bring you long-term happiness.

Controlling the Remote

> When we watch television, my boyfriend and I have blazing fights over who's got the remote control. It drives me mad when he flicks through channels all the time and insists on holding on to it all evening. Friends of mine say their boyfriends do this too. Is it a man thing? What's the best way to encourage him to share the remote?

The TV remote has attracted much attention from sociologists, psychologists, and media researchers. What looks like a functional piece of plastic has been studied as a modern extension of the "male role of hunter-gatherer" and as a potent symbol of female oppression—with batteries. David Morley's 1986 study looked at the viewing habits of eighteen working-class and lower-middle-class families in London. He found that men were more likely than women to plan what they were going to watch in the evening and that their tight grip on the remote control was symbolic of their control over the choice of shows. Women often complained that their husbands would change channels without asking, something they rarely did themselves. Morley was sure that these findings would not be replicated in the other middle classes—he was wrong. A 2004 YouGov poll of 4,118 adults found that the majority felt that men (usually Dad) still ruled the remote control. Researchers have been interested in whether control over the remote represents control over the rest of a couple's relationship. You may have already figured this out. Anecdotally there are stories of men sneaking remotes into their pockets whenever they have to leave the room. Does this oppression know no bounds? In 1993, the journalist Ellen Goodman went so far as to call the remote "the most reactionary implement currently used to undermine equality in modern marriage."

Perhaps men just find it comforting to keep the control nearby. A survey of thirty-six people published in the *Journal of Marriage and Family* found that men most commonly had the remote on the seat or arm of their chair. This allowed them to do things with it that irritated their wives and girlfriends. Women were more likely than men to complain about channel surfing and failing to turn back quickly enough after switching during a commercial break. Only a third of couples shared the remote.

Surveys show that men and women have clear differences in their television viewing preferences; although who hasn't seen her man sneakily watch the odd makeover show? Women traditionally prefer soap operas, while men go for factual programming. Women will often chat or multitask while watching television; men are more likely to watch in concentrated silence.

If your relationship is otherwise happy, you should be able to negotiate the remote control issue. Removing the batteries is only a temporary solution, buying another television is admitting defeat, breaking up even more so. Agree on what you both want to watch and vow never to change the channel without asking first. You *could* buy remote blockers, but he's likely to run off with those too.

Sex and Lies

> My boyfriend has had sex with fewer people than I
> have. We've been together for two months, and I've
> underplayed how many men I've slept with (it's six-
> teen; he's only mentioned sleeping with six women),
> because I don't expect him to be thrilled. If he asks
> me outright, I'll say eight, but he might find out later
> that there were more. What should I do?

You could argue that your boyfriend *should* know the number of men you've slept with, because in order to love you he has to love your past. But I wouldn't argue that. I'm more of the persuasion that says, "Why rub his nose in it?" This is because knowing your partner's entire sexual history, unless it's rele-vant (for example, if a person has never had sex before, or has been sexually abused), will not enhance your relationship. You should still be honest about the sex you've had—just don't be an accountant about it. If arithmetical discrepancies come up later, you can either show surprise that he's forgotten what you told him or tell him that it's in the past and none of his business.

If you go for an underestimate, you won't be alone. Statis-ticians say that the average number of sexual partners men and women have (in a population) should be similar. Yet men frequently say they have two to four times as many sexual partners as women do. Men are more likely than women to visit prostitutes (who usually don't volunteer for sexual sur-veys and may have, according to a paper in the *Proceedings of the National Academy of Sciences*, over six hundred partners a year), but researchers are divided over whether this can explain the math. According to the Centers for Disease Control and Prevention, men aged between thirty and forty-four claim to have had an average of six to eight sexual partners, whereas women of the same age say they have had four. A 2002 poll by London's *Observer* newspaper of 1,027 adults produced an average of seven partners for women and thirteen for men. A 2005 survey of 2,065 heterosexual women and men conducted by the University of Alberta, Canada, came up with 8.6 for women and 31.9 for men. The Alberta researchers suggest that when stating how many partners they've had, men roughly estimate (which means overestimate) while women count carefully (and forget some).

Women may also still feel the chill of a double standard. They are certainly less likely than men to boast about the number of sexual partners and more likely to "forget" meaningless or particularly bad sex. Women generally do not want to be thought of as promiscuous. To test this hypothesis, researchers from the University of Maine performed a rather devious experiment. They divided 201 college students into various groups, telling one group that the sexual survey results would remain anonymous and a second that the researcher might have a look; participants in a third group had electrodes attached to them and were told they were hooked up to a lie detector. Women who thought their answers might be read gave an average of 2.6 partners; those who thought their responses were anonymous said 3.4; while the poor women attached to the lie detector admitted to 4.4 partners. Men's answers hardly varied.

Your sexual past is indeed part of who you are—but most of us edit our past. Some research published in *Psychology Today* reported that while men are happy to tell researchers how many women they've slept with, they too forget some notches on their bedposts when it comes to telling their girlfriends.

Kiss Off

The other day, my girlfriend said that she didn't like how I kiss her. It sounds stupid, but her remark really upset me. We didn't really talk about it, and I'm embarrassed to bring up the subject again. Is there much variation in kissing, and what do most people like?

When I was a teenager, none of my friends wanted to kiss James (the name has been changed to prevent the same hurt feelings that you have) because his tongue penetrated so far into your mouth that he made you gag and, worse, it was all wet and darted around like a snake. It's an oversight of nature that kissing, which exists in almost all cultures, is not an activity we're all naturally good at. Some of us suspect this and practice on mirrors or our own forearms from a young age. But kissing yourself is like trying to tickle yourself—it doesn't work. And who knows if what you're doing is pleasurable to someone else?

People do have opinions on kissing techniques. Researchers at the University of Albany in New York published a study in *Evolutionary Psychology* in which they analyzed answers from 162 male and 308 female psychology students and looked at various aspects of kissing, such as whether it increases sexual arousal (only if done well, you'd guess) and whether people use it to assess each other as relationship material. I'm not sure if I agree with some of the hypotheses (can men really assess female fertility through what they taste when they're kissing?—I think not), but the results sound right. The researchers found that men generally preferred wetter kisses, more tongue contact, and open mouths. They preferred to slip their tongues in first—perhaps it's a territory thing. Men tended to think that kisses directly lead to sex, although some were happy to skip kissing altogether, with just over half saying they would have sex without kissing first. More women than men generally rated kissing as more important, both during sex and throughout relationships. They were also more interested in the state of their kissing partner's teeth than men were.

Kissing may not have the evolutionary significance that it used to as a way of tasting someone and seeing how healthy they are (as the authors of the study suggest), but it's important that the other party likes how you kiss. In a separate survey done by one of the authors, 58 men and 122 women were asked if they'd ever found someone attractive but had been put off after kissing them. A total of 59 percent of men and 66 percent of women said yes. If you don't want to quiz your partner on how she likes being kissed, you could, based on this study's findings, try less saliva and tongue penetration and a slower, more relaxed approach. In her book *Kissing*, the kissing expert Andrea Demirjian offers the following tips for a good kiss: a clean mouth, a bit of anticipation, some sucking and biting of lips (theirs), and a relaxed tongue. To which I would add: not too wet and let them come up for air.

I Was Only Saying . . .

I come from a family where my parents never argued, but my girlfriend and I have quite a few arguments, often over little things. Although we shout at each other, our fights are quite short-lived, and we generally get along well. Are relationships better if you never argue?

If a couple never argues, it doesn't mean they have a great relationship. They may be uninterested in what their significant other has to say. In which case what's there to argue about? This isn't to say your parents weren't happy, but arguing is not necessarily a barometer of how good or bad a relationship is. The research suggests that it's okay to argue if you do so in a civilized manner. Conflict is normal in relationships; it's how you deal with it that determines how damaging it is.

According to the UK research organization One Plus One, most couples argue over money, feeling jealous, who does the housework, and communication ("You never talk to me, so let's argue about it"). If you had children, they would also land on the list. And how often do couples argue? A survey of sixty couples (who had been seeing each other for at least five months) published in the journal *Family Relations* found that they argued on average nearly five times in two weeks. The arguments that made men most unhappy with their relationship were ones that came up again and again; the ones that made women unhappy were over issues they felt never got resolved. You can see the problem.

You may think having a civilized argument misses the point, but verbal weaponry can be immensely destructive. While sticks and stones may be needed to break bones, words can lay waste to your relationship. Researchers warn that contempt, sarcasm, and aggression—the main ingredients of many fine arguments—are very hard to recover from. Name-calling or anything that comes close to verbal abuse is a spectacularly bad idea. If you can, keep an argument at low intensity and try to negotiate. Avoid storing up ammunition in one fight for use in future arguments, or you will never get over anything, ever. Stick to the issue and do not drag in stuff you're still annoyed about from three years ago. Have some idea of what you want the outcome to be; don't argue just because there is nothing good on television. Couples who have serious problems will have arguments that are openly hostile and cruel. This type of arguing never makes a relationship better.

Quality arguments are ended either by someone saying "sorry" (this is a great healer of relationships, but you must feel sorry as well as say the word), or by the couple mutually agreeing upon a solution. The most damaging are ended by one person stomping out or withdrawing emotionally. A study of seventy-nine married couples published in the *Journal of Marriage and Family* found that men were most distressed when their spouses withdrew from them after an argument, especially if they acted as if they didn't care about them anymore (such as wandering off when their husband was trying to tell them about a bad day at work). Women were most upset when their husbands got angry and sarcastic.

The only way to never argue is to ignore any conflict, and most studies show that this doesn't make for happy relationships. You can be a happy couple and argue; just do it with dignity, stick to the issue, say "sorry" afterward, and mean it.

4

What Happens Next?

Going the Distance

I'm English, and I've been seeing an American guy for six months. His work is taking him home, and although we don't want to break up, we're not at the "let's stay together forever" stage. We want to try to carry on our relationship even though it will be over a long distance. Can this work, or will it just prolong the agony?

You shouldn't have a long-distance relationship just because you have the opportunity to do so. Only do it if you both want to commit to one. Research shows that optimism in a long-distance relationship, or LDR (as it's called), is an indicator of success, so your concern about potential agony is legitimate. For an LDR to work, you must focus on the positives: having your own social life and career while building a relationship with someone you hope you have a future with.

There's a center for LDRs run by Gregory Guldner, a California doctor. He's optimistic about LDRs, based on a study he carried out from Purdue University comparing two hundred couples in LDRs with two hundred who were "geographically close." He found that couples in LDRs have the same intimacy and commitment in their relationship as those close by each other. He has some good advice for how to go about an LDR, should you choose to do so.

Your biggest fear—and that of most people in LDRs—is that one of you will have an affair. But remember that even people who live together worry about that. Guldner found LDRs had no greater risk of affairs than non-LDRs. Other factors determine whether someone strays, such as the quality of the relationship and how people feel about infidelity (and if they're likely to take up a chance to have opportunistic sex). You ask if LDRs can work at all, presumably because you think they can't last, but some research shows that LDRs are no more likely to break up than other relationships when factors such as age are accounted for. (See the next section, "Homeward Bound," as the evidence suggests that moving back together may even *increase* your chances of breaking up.) Essentially it's the couple's relationship first, the distance second. You are more likely to have an LDR that works if you assume that if things work out you'll at some stage be geographically close again.

There's not much correlation between how often you see or talk to each other and how likely you are to stay together, unless you go for weeks without speaking and never see each other more frequently than in six-month intervals. So what can you do to increase your chances? Set clear rules: when you will speak and meet again, and whether you will go on dates with other people. You wouldn't do this if you lived near each other, but some couples feel it is unrealistic to stay monogamous when they live thousands of miles apart. Guldner's research shows that people in LDRs are good at communicating about deep feelings but forget to talk about their humdrum daily lives. Both are essential for intimacy. So tell him when a friend stands you up or a shop assistant is incredibly rude, but don't invest too much emotion in phone calls. Don't be oversensitive if you hear him yawn or empty the dishwasher. Likewise, if one visit doesn't live up to your expectations, it doesn't mean the next one won't. All relationships have ups and downs. LDRs need to grow—so it's okay to have arguments and think he's a jerk. If you wear rose-tinted glasses, the relationship will die from disillusionment.

Dr. Mary Holmes, from the department of sociology at Flinders University in Adelaide, Australia, conducted a study of fourteen academic couples living apart and confirmed Guldner's findings of emotional closeness in LDRs and the importance of sharing details of daily life. Holmes concluded that relationships could survive physical distance. Those LDRs that work out usually move closer within four years. And moving closer is really the point.

Homeward Bound

My girlfriend and I have had a long-distance relationship for two years. She found out just before Christmas that she got a new job, which means she'll come back to England. We both wanted this to happen, and she'll move in with me. Our relationship has always been romantic, but it will be very different seeing each other every day. Will we be more or less likely to still be together by the end of next year?

One would hope that it's more likely you'd be together after a year, but it's hard to say. LDRs are so romantic and difficult that they deserve "happily ever after" endings. Although there are self-help books and Web sites devoted to LDRs, some studies on LDRs changing back to ordinary relationships are not terribly helpful. This is because they've been carried out with either military or undergraduate couples. Military couples have unique problems, as active service distances you from most people, hence their frequent complaint that their partners feel like strangers. This problem is so common that a Royal Air Force Web site directs people to an LDR site called longdistancecouples.com. We'll look at the undergraduate studies (since they're all we've got), but these people are in their early twenties, while many people in LDRs are older.

Being geographically close should be good because the research says that it is talking about the mundane things, rather than making grand gestures, that makes relationships strong. So not the red roses at the arrivals gate but the conversation that goes, "Now that you're back, it's your week to do the grocery shopping." An Ohio State University paper published in the *Journal of Social and Personal Relationships* found that out of 180 long-distance couples who moved closer, 114 stayed together but 66 broke up, two-thirds of them within the first three months. Most people missed something about their long-distance arrangement: the freedom, novelty value, and special sort of closeness they'd felt while living apart. They were four times as likely to notice a new negative quality in their partner as a positive one, usually laziness and immaturity (but then, they were students). Jealousy, funnily enough, became more common.

This study found that couples who stayed long distance

had the same rate of splitting up as those who moved closer, but another study of undergraduates carried out a year later and published in the same journal found a higher rate in couples who moved closer. It's not clear why there was this difference, but the later study found that LDR couples who were more idealistic about their relationships and had longer gaps between seeing each other were more likely to break up when they moved closer.

Therefore, you need to do a rapid and thorough reality check. This can be difficult while you are in an LDR, because there are so many pressures. In an LDR people are more careful to avoid bickering about the trivial, because time together is short and usually costs money (for example, airfare). In GCRs (geographically close relationships) time is not at such a premium, so you can bicker all day if you want to. In fact, once you become geographically close again, it can seem as though quantity has replaced quality. So you will need to readjust to include your partner in your mundane life and to be tolerant of what proximity unearths about each other. Now what could be more romantic than that?

Faith in Our Relationship

I am a Muslim woman who is about to tell my traditional parents that I plan to marry my white boyfriend. He will convert, and we won't live together beforehand, but even so, they may disown me. Will this and our cultural difference make it less likely for us to survive as a couple?

Do cultural differences and parents who'll disown you make you more likely to break up? There isn't a simple yes or no to this question, as you may have expected. Relationship research shows that like marries like and that the support of family and friends helps keep couples together. There isn't much research (and most of it is outdated) that specifically looks at the risk of divorce among couples of different religious or ethnic groups.

And your situation is, perhaps surprisingly, still unusual. In England and Wales, the latest figures from the Office for National Statistics show that only 2 percent of marriages are between people of different ethnic groups. Among the Bangladeshi population in England and Wales, 3 percent of people marry outside their group. White people are the least likely to marry outside their ethnic group. Even so, in some countries inter-ethnic marriages are rising. For example, in the United States, according to sociologist Michael J. Rosenfeld from Stanford University, inter-ethnic marriages have increased from less than 2 percent in 1970 to over 7 percent in 2007.

But whatever the figures, your parents probably expected to arrange your marriage. This alone will be shocking for them, although they may have noticed differences between their life and yours. The UK National Survey of Ethnic Minorities (admittedly in the 1990s) found that most people in South Asian communities had their spouses chosen for them by their parents, although even ten years ago people under the age of thirty-four were more likely than older people to want to choose their own partner.

The evidence for break-ups is conflicting but is likely to become clearer with more research. As ethnic and religious groups integrate, they become more likely to marry people from other ethnic and religious groups. Studies of divorce rates have tended to list rather than analyze the reasons. Research from Germany found mixed marriages (except those between German women and Turkish or Yugoslav men) had no higher divorce rates. A study (twenty years old) looking at 10 percent of divorces in California found shorter marriages between Afro-Caribbean men and white women (by nearly two years). An Australian study in the *Journal of Marriage and Family* found, by reanalyzing data from a study of marriages in Hawaii, that mixed marriages did have higher divorce rates but argued that these were due to the beliefs that different ethnic groups have about divorce. If you are from an ethnic group that disapproves of divorce, that will reduce your risk no matter whom you marry.

There are likely to be additional factors at work, but other studies show that marriages where one partner has converted to the other's religion have lower than average divorce rates. (The evidence is strongest among people who convert to the Jewish faith.) Conversion is also more likely to encourage family and friends to embrace the relationship.

Although I don't want to underestimate the struggle ahead, the fundamentals of long-lasting relationships are romance, companionship, love, support, and loyalty. You have to believe that these things cross cultural boundaries.

Toy Boy or Not Toy Boy?

I've always been out with men who were my age or a couple of years older. I broke up with someone I'd been living with, and it's taken me four years to meet someone I really care about. The problem is he's seven years younger than me. I'm thirty-five. We've talked about getting married. Is this age gap too trivial to worry about?

There's a lot of mythology around age differences in relationships. Such relationships are more diverse than you'd think.

The Office for National Statistics in England and Wales defines the age gap in marriages as the husband's age minus the wife's age. This reflects the most common pattern and is why you feel a bit uneasy. To some extent you're as old as you behave, but it's hard for couples to have the same values, interests, and energy levels if their ages are too disparate. It's going to cause tensions if a woman midmenopause meets a twenty-five-year-old man who wants his own children (although she can use the services of a fertility doctor). Even so, marriage statistics show a surprising range in age differences. Three-quarters of marriages are between couples where the woman is between four years older to eight years younger than her man, which leaves a good quarter who have an age gap that's bigger. Your relationship has a –7 age gap, which doesn't seem that much off the scale, especially at your ages.

You're actually being quite conformist; more women are marrying younger men in countries as diverse as the United States and Korea. The proportion of couples in the United Kingdom where the husband was younger than his wife increased from 15 percent in 1963 to 26 percent in 2003. Women are more likely to marry younger men if they've been married before. The UK Office for National Statistics is clear that the age distribution actually reflects indifference (its word) to the age of our partners. An American Association of Retired Persons survey of 3,500 single people between the ages of forty and sixty found that 34 percent of women over forty are dating younger men (but it didn't say how much younger). The term "cougar" is often used to describe older women who date younger men—a reference to the cat's predatory nature.

A revolution in social norms isn't happening, but gradually the stereotype of a handful of dysfunctional younger men wanting older women because it's the nearest they'll get to having sex with their mom and because they can sponge off her larger salary is being eroded. It's becoming more mainstream for perfectly normal men to date older women. As long ago as 1999, a study in the journal *Family Planning Perspectives* discussed data showing that among women up to the age of forty-five (the researchers were looking at pregnancy really, which is why they stopped at forty-five), 29 percent had a partner who was three to five years older and 7 percent had one who was six years or more older. A study at California State College found that people believed that relationships with large age gaps of around, for example, eighteen years were less likely to succeed but were very hopeful about what they called "moderate" gaps of seven years.

Even better, there's research from the University of Oklahoma showing that women married to younger men (by six or more years) live longer than those married to older men. So you'll have more years to enjoy your relationship.

My Valentine

> I'm planning to ask my gorgeous girlfriend to marry me on Valentine's Day. (We've been together for two years.) She complains that I'm not romantic, so I thought I'd surprise her with dinner at a lovely restaurant and a ring. But now I'm getting cold feet—that it's not romantic but cheesy. Which is it?

Is it cheesy to ask someone to marry you on Valentine's Day? Surveys show that over 60 percent of people would find it romantic. If it's not too much of a surprise and your girlfriend wants to marry you, she is likely to be thrilled wherever you ask her. What's not to like about someone saying they love you and want to spend the rest of their life with you (unless she's got other plans)?

Rather than worrying about being cheesy, you should worry about being old-fashioned. Don't you know that these days many people are opting to live together without marrying? So you must believe in celebrating commitment, as being married may not make any difference financially. And in this cynical world, that makes you seriously romantic.

Proposing is still a key part of the marriage tradition, so give some thought to how you do the asking. A Good Morning Television (GMTV) survey of over 8,500 people found that in the United Kingdom two-thirds of marriages started with a formal proposal—still overwhelmingly by men. Most surveys of attitudes toward proposing and Valentine's Day come from companies with a vested interest: jewelers, florists, and condom manufacturers. (The latter conducted a survey showing what women most wanted on Valentine's Day was sex.) You don't need to get down on one knee; a jeweler's survey of fifty thousand Americans found that two-thirds of people thought it unnecessary (though younger people in this survey, between the ages of eighteen and thirty-four, were twice as likely to want to propose on bended knee as older people—presumably because they're still flexible enough to get up afterward). You don't have to present an engagement ring, as women often like to choose it, and like underwear it's embarrassing if it's too tight.

If you want general tips on how to be more romantic, the surveys all point to personal touch beating the grand gesture. Romance is about small acts of kindness. An online survey of 250 Americans found that most preferred a handpicked bunch of wildflowers to twelve long-stemmed out-of-season roses and that women find the following overwhelmingly romantic: their partner doing household chores, cooking them a meal, and thoughtfulness such as, "Are you cold? Why don't you borrow my jacket?" You also need to think about whether you want to propose privately or make a more public gesture. A *Psychology Today* survey of 250 people found that just over a third would be turned off by a proposal on television or in skywriting or at a public venue. I'm surprised it's not more.

Insurance companies have done their own Valentine's Day surveys. Engagement rings in champagne glasses (glug glug, choke), proposing on top of and then sliding off mountains, and all those candle-lit (oops, my hair's alight) suppers bring many claims. So be aware that romantic gestures have many risks. The likelihood of being turned down is probably the least of them.

Stop or Shop

My girlfriend and I are buying a house and are about to sign the contract. We've been together for two years and now virtually live in my apartment, but for the last month we haven't been getting along very well. We don't fight; we just barely talk to each other. Usually I'm the one to reach out and apologize, so I expect I'll do it this time. But should we still be moving in together since we're getting on so badly?

Buying a house can put stress on even the strongest relationships, so a month of tension midpurchase may be reversible. But not if you don't talk to each other. Are you investing in a future together or just buying a property? Did you discuss that future before you applied for a joint mortgage? Thirty years ago, living together out of wedlock was frowned upon; until recently it was usually a prelude to marriage. Now it's an end in itself. The figures for how long people who live together stay together are worse than for people in marriages, but they also reflect how casually some couples decide to cohabit (whether or not they buy property together). Cohabitation has become so much the norm that it's hard to know whether most couples think it's any more significant than going on vacation together.

So why do most couples move in together? A study by Dr. Sharon Sassler from Ohio State University asked twenty-five people (between the ages of twenty and thirty-three and living in New York) who had lived together for three months why they'd done so, and found that less than a third had ever discussed their future together. Over half moved in together quite rapidly—within six months. Some said this was because they were so attracted to each other and spent so much time together that merging households just happened. But these reasons were largely translated into more practical ones: moving in together to save money and for convenience. Do either of these sound familiar?

Data from the British Household Panel Survey show that 70 percent of first relationships are cohabitations (and not marriage) and that these last on average two years. They're mostly experimental (as in, "Just how much will we save on the gas bill?") and never meant to be long-term. As with the New York couples, they often happen because so much time is spent together that migration into one or the other's home seems like a natural progression. But two years is only an average; there are cohabiting relationships that last a lifetime. Mostly these started out with the intention of being together forever. Increasingly, cohabiting relationships will last longer because they will be chosen by more people over marriage.

You may not have needed to brush up on your conflict

resolution skills before now because you were still in the throes of being easily pleased. But for a future together, you can't fall apart over buying a house. Worse things will happen. There's a huge body of research on withdrawal behavior (sulking) in response to conflict, and it basically says: sulking sucks. Intimacy avoidance, as psychologists call it, is the antithesis of what's needed when the going gets tough. The point of being together (apart from the sex and being able to afford a better property) is to emotionally support each other. So start talking about your future and how you're going to deal with the problems you're bound to have together *before* signing on to anything as significant as a house.

He's Not the One

> My girlfriend says she loves me but she's not sure if I'm her soul mate, and because of this she wants to wait before we move in together. I think she means she's not sure that we have a future, or am I being too sensitive? Do people really believe in soul mates?

People really do believe in soul mates, in finding someone who is "the one" for them. Soul mates usually are romantic partners but can, according to various "soul mate" books, include friends, siblings, or even children. Soul mates can be identified by their ability to talk to you for hours on first meeting, to understand you better than your mother does, and to be able to finish your sentences for you. Life with a soul mate is meant to be easy and natural and take place in a thatched cottage. No wonder so many people want to know where to find one. The answer should be somewhere nearby, as soul mates usually have a similar background; hence their ability to know you so well.

The pursuit of a soul mate is a relatively modern phenomenon, although Plato is credited with sowing the seeds. He writes in his *Symposium* that humans once had four legs, four arms, and two faces but were cut in half by the god Zeus, who feared their power. The halves have been trying to find each other ever since.

The idea is now so pervasive that a Gallup survey of 1,003 young American adults ages twenty to twenty-nine found that 94 percent of the single ones (the actual numbers for singles are not given) believed that "when you marry you want your spouse to be your soul mate, first and foremost." Nearly 90 percent of them also thought "there is a special person, a soul mate, waiting for you somewhere out there." Most of them also thought they'd find them. Nearly as many thought the divorce rate was too high. Which begs the question, Is there a correlation here?

The problem with the "only a soul mate will do" philosophy is that it carries a promise of an effortless, perfect relationship. Relationships based on "we're soul mates" carry a risk of someone bailing out when no one wants to take out the trash or get out of bed for a screaming toddler.

Dr. Neil Clark Warren set up eHarmony, the online dating and matching service, using the research he conducted on marriages. He defined twenty-nine dimensions of compatibility for happy marriages and says that to meet a soul mate you have to look beyond the usual five desirable qualities of looks, chemistry, a sense of humor, a good personality, and some financial security. Does your potential soul mate have a dysfunctional family? (Doesn't everyone?) Do you have the same energy level? Does your mate like being alone? How does he or she deal with disagreements? Essentially, Warren's point is that soul mates make for compatible partners, but you need to check thoroughly and go for some objective evidence of compatibility rather than going on some fuzzy feeling that this person can read your mind.

Your girlfriend may mean that you're not "the one," or that she doesn't know yet. Ask her what she means by a soul mate and how well she thinks you're matched. If she isn't sure, work on getting to know each other better. What you can't do is pretend to be her soul mate, because your own soul is unlikely to go along with it.

Getting to "Yes"

> My boyfriend has never had relationships lasting longer than a year. He really pursued me, but after eight months he's blowing more hot and cold, saying he's busy, that I'm not like he thought I was, and that he's not sure he's ready for a serious relationship. Is there anything I can do to make him feel more committed to me, or am I just not the one for him?

You can only get a commitment phobe to commit if he wants to. And if he wanted to, he wouldn't be phobic, would he? Commitment phobes look normal (they won't be wearing running shoes for swift retreats) but have a history that gives them away. Watch out for a history of brief relationships (those no longer than a year) or an accelerated pursuit that may seem flattering but can't be well thought out, since he can't know much about you so early on. When you then decide (often out of exhaustion) to give it a try and act like a girlfriend, commitment phobes swiftly withdraw. They may also become rather critical, usually picking on something you can't change easily such as your family or the shape of your ears.

The commitment phobe can be confused with the total bastard, but commitment phobia is a more clearly defined condition. Women can have it, though the term "commitment phobia" was invented for men, coined in 1987 by Steven Carter in a book based on interviews with fifty women called *Men Who Can't Love*. Carter nearly called it the Houdini syndrome, after all the men he'd been told about who'd vanished from relationships (one left a Rome hotel for cigarettes and never returned). Carter defined a behavioral pattern in commitment phobes of pursuit and panic, although he doesn't say why it occurs, preferring to make it clear to women that it's not their fault and that they should get out before their self-esteem disappears along with their partner.

Commitment is usually defined in terms of dedication to your partner and some self-sacrificing element that involves your putting the greater good of the relationship above your own grubby needs. In return, commitment, so the research says, makes you happier, healthier, and more resilient to life's occasional thwacks. If you want to know how commitment develops, there's plenty of research to tell you. A study of one hundred male and ninety-nine female students by researchers at Indiana University Northwest, published in the *Journal of Social and Personal Relationships*, asked people what they'd done to change a casual relationship into a serious one. Nearly 40 percent said they'd seen their partner more and for longer periods of time, nearly 30 percent said they started talking about how they felt about their relationships, and 26 percent made the relationship more intense by asking for support or personal advice. About 16 percent asked outright for a more serious relationship. Other studies also show that it's the degree of commitment that men have that decides how positively they view their partner.

If your partner does not exhibit any of the behavior in the first study, he may not want commitment, and if he doesn't want commitment, the other studies suggest he doesn't value you highly and may be sniffing around for alternatives.

I'm guessing here, but 100 percent of men who don't want to commit won't do so. They may move in, marry, have kids with you, but these are events and not commitments. For the commitment-phobic partner, hyperventilating at the thought of being together forever, neither you nor anyone else is ever going to be the one, unless they are a trained therapist.

Marry without Haste

My girlfriend and I have lived together for eight years and have one child. We've decided to get married, but she's read that people who live together first are more likely to divorce than those who haven't. (We know couples who have experienced this.) Should we stay as we are?

In the United States, one-third of babies in 2007 were born to unmarried couples—an increase of 5 percent from 1960. According to the Council on Contemporary Families, 80 percent of such couples are living together when they have their babies but five years after the babies are born, only a quarter of the parents are married and half have broken up. But these figures include a wide variety of couples, some of whom never intended to have children or stay together.

Living together is a mainstream activity, and over 80 percent of couples who get married nowadays will have lived together first. Much of the research into whether cohabiting first increases your chances of breaking up after you marry was done in the 1980s and '90s when such couples were more unconventional and living in sin raised eyebrows. This research showed that couples who live together are less happy, more unfaithful, less confident about their relationships, and more abusive to each other than married folk. It also showed that they were twice as likely to divorce as couples who didn't live together first. Men in particular were less committed to cohabiting relationships than to married ones.

Why isn't living together a good preparation for marriage? Some researchers speculate that couples carry their lower commitment levels into a casual attitude toward marriage. One day they wake up and say, "We need some new kitchen stuff, let's get married so we can put it on our wedding registry." When the going gets tough, this casual approach becomes, "Let's get divorced." Simplistic? You'd have to think so.

It may be that couples who embraced living together in the 1970s and 1980s were different from the cohabiting couples of today. An Australian study published in *Family Matters* in 2003 found that modern cohabiting couples who later married stayed together at rates similar to those for couples who married straight off. This study was unusual because time together was measured from when the couples first got together, whereas in older studies it was measured from the wedding. When the researchers took into consideration other risk factors for divorce, such as youth, poverty, having parents who'd divorced, and lower educational levels, the difference fell to 5 percent after eight years of marriage—still significant, but smaller. Today it would be those who didn't live together first who'd be the odd couples. Yet there may still be a risk of what researchers (from the University of Denver in a paper in *Family Relations*) call a "slide rather than a decide into marriage," which makes some marriages that started off as cohabiting relationships more vulnerable. In the United States, the Marriage Project cites a 1992 study of 3,300 couples that found those who had lived together beforehand had a 46 percent increase in divorces.

But John Ermisch, a statistician at the University of Essex in England who has studied cohabitation, says that when studies take into account the other risk factors for divorce, the risks are eliminated or even reversed. So there is no compelling evidence to stop you from getting married. Only the cost and arguing about the guest list.

Love Match Has Catch

> My parents have said I do not have to have an arranged marriage if I don't want to, but I know it will hurt them deeply if I don't. I am unsure what to do. My parents' generation think that arranged marriages are more successful than love matches. What should I do?

Many people still have arranged marriages, especially in Asia, Africa, and the Middle East. It's estimated that around 90 percent of marriages in India are arranged. Now that divorce rates are nudging over 33 percent in some Western countries, arranged marriages have attracted some interest in the West, but they have also had bad press, being associated with forced marriages and childhood betrothals. Historically, arranged marriages were for the social and economic advancement of families rather than the benefit of individuals. Men were typically older than their wives (and sometimes frankly ancient), and couples were matched for religious belief, caste (where it existed), money, looks (taller men only, please), and the social standing of each family.

Arguments for arranged marriages are based on the perception that young people are impulsive and will choose a romantic partner for superficial reasons such as looks and sexual chemistry. The intense and unrealistic feelings in "love matches" are bashed by the reality of child rearing and laundry. This causes many to bail out or become progressively unhappy. Arranged marriages are said to "start cold and heat up." There are no expectations of happiness, but a duty felt to the families and matchmakers who have brought them together, so working at the relationship is a given. But at the risk of being trivial, you could marry someone you will never find sexually attractive, which is becoming increasingly unacceptable for many young people who are expected to have arranged marriages. Which may be partly why, as you probably know, the arranged marriage market has lightened up. Amit Batabyal, professor of economics at the Rochester Institute of Technology in New York, has researched the economics of arranged marriages and says that modern ones are more flexible. Parents and matchmakers are more like consultants than marriage enforcers, suggesting rather than insisting on a partner.

You'd hope that an arranged marriage would reduce your risk of divorce and make you happier. Batabyal says divorce rates are higher in countries with mostly love matches, but this may be because economic and political factors prevent divorce in countries where arranged marriages prevail. A report in the *Times of India* says that divorce rates in Mumbai are 40 percent. According to another report in the *Times of India*, divorce rates are rising in Goa, although the numbers there seem small, at 384 a year. The Web site divorcerate.org says that India's divorce rate is still around 1 percent.

So are arranged marriages any happier? A study of 586 married women in Sichuan in China compared those who'd had love matches with those in arranged marriages by asking them how satisfied they were with their relationships. It found women in love matches were happier than those in arranged marriages. Both types of marriage were rated more highly the longer the marriage lasted.

If you are the first generation to try a love match, it will be hard for your parents. You may want to try a half-and-half approach, whereby they suggest people but you don't have to marry them. Agree with them on what you will do if you meet someone yourself and what you are looking for. Try to avoid falling for too unusual a choice, as this may be too much for most parents to deal with.

What's in a Name?

My boyfriend and I are getting married. Our relationship is based on love and equality. Our marriage raises the question of sharing a surname. By giving up my surname, I fear I will lose part of my identity and feel subordinated to my boyfriend. Using the same name has practical advantages (more so if we have children), but I cannot help seeing this as an expression of male dominance. My boyfriend likes the idea of one surname but thinks it should be his because it's easier to spell (English) and mine is Dutch. How do other women deal with this problem?

It comes down to personal choice. You can keep your maiden name; take his surname and use your maiden name as a middle name; mesh your names to form a new one (for example,

Williams marrying Smithson becomes Wilson—why not have both parties lose their identity?); take his surname legally but use your maiden name; or, the most radical option, he could take your name. Confused? Well, you can see why most women go the traditional route—around 90 percent according to a study at the Millikin University in Illinois published in the journal *Sex Roles*. This seems to be the case around the world based on the findings in a paper called "The Surname of Married Women in the European Union" in *Population and Societies*, although there are variations. In Italy, for example, women often use both surnames.

Generally, taking the husband's name is a family pleaser (his family is usually the most pleased), some say it's romantic, and if you have children you'll be known by their surname anyway. If you choose your husband's surname, you will automatically defuse the potentially huge minefield of what surname you put on your children's birth certificates. Some women, however, are opposed to endorsing a patriarchal practice dating from a time when husbands had all the power. If it makes you feel too uncomfortable, don't do it. However, you will still have to cope with people you don't know very well assuming you have adopted your husband's surname.

Traditionally, if you take your husband's surname, you get his whole name. As Mrs. John Smith, you are completely subordinated—you'll have disappeared. But, thankfully, few use this convention today.

Some women are more likely to keep their own surname than others. A study in the *Journal of Economic Perspectives* on women's surnames by researchers at Harvard University found that women graduates from Harvard were more likely to keep their surnames if they had higher degrees, jobs in the arts or media, and longer careers before marriage. Out of a total of 390 married women in the class of 1980, 44 percent kept their surname; compared to 32 percent in 1990 (no actual numbers were given for 1990). The authors speculate that keeping your surname is now less of a feminist issue.

Most women try their spouse's name on for size (how does Mrs. Emma Roydes sound?). Most research shows women feel either neutral or positive about taking their husband's surname. You may not. Only you can answer the question, What's in a name? From what you've said, it sounds like there's a lot.

Looking Good?

> My partner is much better looking than I am. I'm not exactly ugly, but he's so attractive that people comment on it and I see women drooling over him. He seems oblivious to it, but I wonder if the relationship is doomed because he's so good-looking that people will come on to him all the time. Is our relationship less likely to last?

The stereotype is of a beautiful woman going out with a less attractive man, so you're correct in thinking your connection is unconventional. Some people would tell you to shut up and stop being so superficial, but not me. This is because the research shows that people choose romantic partners who are similar to them—even in the looks department. A study called "Facial Resemblance in Engaged and Married Couples," published in the *Journal of Social and Personal Relationships*, hypothesized that couples look like each other because, according to psychological theory, repeated exposure to a stimulus (your face in the mirror) makes that stimulus more attractive. This translates into "If you look like me, you're gorgeous." In this study psychology students (who you'd think would have guessed what the study was trying to show) rated the similarity of male to female faces in sixty paired photographs. About half of the pairs were either engaged or married; the others were randomly put together. The real couples were rated as more similar in standard measures of attractiveness, such as how symmetrical their face was and how prominent their cheekbones were (think Balkan supermodel).

If you have defied the laws of nature and are with a person much better looking than you, what will happen? Reducing your relationship to a mercenary transaction, you may have other things that make you attractive to him: conversation, affection, stability, or money. If your relationship is just about looks, the research doesn't bode well. A 1980s study from the University of Maryland compared attractiveness levels in 123 couples (on a nine-point scale) and gave them a thirty-five-page relationship questionnaire. They found that couples in the most serious relationships were more likely to be of similar attractiveness. Nine months later, those who were less similar were more likely to have broken up. Men who were more attractive (regardless of how good-looking their partner was) were more likely to admit to thinking about other relationships (except those who were married).

Most of the research has looked at levels of attractiveness early on in relationships. A study from the University of California in Los Angeles delved deeper into the influence that levels of attractiveness have in more established relationships. James McNulty and his colleagues analyzed how eighty-three couples, on average together for forty-five months, discussed a personal problem, while researchers ranked the facial attractiveness of each person. The research team found that the more attractive husbands were less supportive of their wives, especially when their wives were less attractive than they were. This, they concluded, was because good-looking men have their pick of women and may be less ready to be satisfied and supportive in their own relationships. As they admitted, however, such a conclusion is mere speculation; the study showed an association, not proof that good-looking men are bastards.

It's also worth knowing that other studies show we over-estimate how attractive our partners really are (and how likely our relationships are to last forever)—such are the positive illusions that love brings. That said, your partner's looks seem to be an issue for you, and you'll need to deal with it. He's chosen to be with you, so instead of insisting you don't believe him, enjoy his looks and see if his personality is just as attractive.

Jealousy and Affairs

Men in Uniform

My partner and I have been together for six years, and after three he joined the police. Friends of ours are full of stories of affairs. I trust my partner and we're planning our wedding, but is there evidence that working in a tight-knit group over unsocial hours induces affairs?

It's hard to know how reliable the statistics are on how many people have affairs at work. When the company Human and Legal Resources conducted a survey of 1,072 employees from different industries, it found that 61 percent had had affairs at work and one-third of these people were already married. Most affairs occurred in the leisure and tourism industry and the least in health care. This doesn't tell us much, because both types of jobs can involve long hours, but arguably it's more stressful being a doctor than a travel agent. There's good evidence that unsocial hours cause unhappiness in relationships; a study of 1,668 married couples by the University of Nebraska-Lincoln found the risk of divorce increased from 7 percent to 11 percent over the three years of the study (which was statistically significant). Other surveys suggest that if you work long hours, surrounded by members of the opposite sex, you may be susceptible to an affair. But it depends on the person's views on infidelity and their existing relationship.

There are no national statistics linking occupation and divorce, because they aren't routinely collected by statistics offices. There are no employment questions on divorce papers. There is some rampant mythology around police marriages; one U.S. Web site quotes a 75 percent divorce rate, and another a rate seven times higher than average, comparable, it says, to doctors' divorce rates. But there is good evidence that rates are not higher than average among doctors, so the statistics on police divorces may not be reliable either. A study published in the *New England Journal of Medicine* of 1,118 married doctors found that only certain specialties, such as psychiatry, had slightly higher rates. Both doctors and policemen look after the public, but in a direct comparison of attractiveness police officers may win because of the uniform and handcuffs.

Researchers from the University of California, Berkeley, looked at the effects of stress at work on nineteen male police officers and their wives, asking them to keep thirty-day stress diaries and watching them interact in a laboratory. The researchers were looking for the early warning signs of an imploding relationship (for example, the inability of a couple to regulate their emotions and remain civil to each other). They found that although the police officers were stressed, their wives tried very hard to be civil to them. Couples did cope because both partners supported each other. The researchers were clear, however, that continued job stress is toxic for relationships.

Dr. Ellen Kirschman, a psychologist who is an expert on police officers and relationships, says they do not have more affairs or divorces than anyone else. Cops are psychologically screened and so should start their careers at least above average in tests that screen for mental health.

You can forget about affairs as potential flash points. Kirschman says that police officers are more likely to damage their relationships by being distant emotionally and anxious about the vulnerability of their family (bringing their work home with them). It's this that can be hard to live with.

New Company

My girlfriend has a new job in a big company that is known for socializing after work. We've been together (happily) for three years, but now she'll meet new men and go out drinking more at this job than at her old one. Am I being insecure in worrying that I'll lose her?

Opportunity is a risk factor for infidelity but not the foregone conclusion you think it is. The many studies on infidelity show that it depends on three main factors. They sound rather premeditated, but it's certain that your girlfriend won't be using them as a conscious checklist. First, it depends on how likely she is to think she can find someone better than you. Second, it depends on how much she has invested and thus can lose in your relationship, and finally it depends on her beliefs on infidelity. Most people (in the United States, Gallup polls consistently show over 90 percent) disapprove of infidelity, especially in long-standing relationships. But around a quarter of people will be unfaithful and rationalize it in various ways—being unfulfilled (that is, not having enough sex), or being underwhelmed by their partner, overwhelmed by someone else, or under the influence. For many people it really is an inconsequential act; it only ceases to be if you, the partner, find out about it.

The UK Sexual Attitudes and Lifestyles Survey found that women who work are three times more likely to be unfaithful to a partner than those who stay at home (where they only meet postmen and plumbers). Other studies show an increase among people who travel overnight for work (hotels have sex appeal), those who are less happy in their relationship, and those who have been unfaithful before. Studies in the United States show that the availability of eligible partners does increase the likelihood of infidelity, especially where women work in areas where they are outnumbered by men. Some American companies have tried to ban relationships at work and made it clear that if people hook up at work they must tell their bosses and one of them should find another job. Clearly, affairs at work do happen, and a survey by the company Human and Legal Resources of 1,072 workers found that 61 percent had had an office romance, and in a third of these romances one or both partners were married. There is evidence from other studies that the likelihood of an affair depends on the availability of partners. A Swedish study found that the divorce rate was 70 percent higher for a person whose coworkers were all members of the opposite sex. The sex ratios at work are likely to be more influential on rates of couples breaking up than forming in the first place.

But this doesn't mean your girlfriend has any desire to stray. If she's committed to you, she won't send out or accept messages of availability. Psychologists do have suggestions on how to affair-proof relationships that sound nauseating but work better than the only other alternative (sabotaging your partner's career): you have to have a conversation for at least forty minutes every day, go on regular dates each week, and be affectionate. You could suggest meeting her after work sometimes, but stop being insecure—it will look desperate. The odds are against her cheating with someone else, so your insecurity, happily, is likely to be unnecessary.

Is She Faithful?

> I think my girlfriend is having an affair. She's been working closely with a man whom I've never liked, because he's known to be lecherous, and she's been coming home very late some nights. She's definitely more distant. Should I ask her outright or snoop around?

The choice is yours. There's a whole industry feeding people's need to know if their significant other is cheating. Some people may worry with good reason; others will be vulnerable because they're insecure. If you want proof, you can try anything from online kits to private detectives and sophisticated surveillance techniques that tell you every move your partner makes on her computer and the calls she's deleted from her cell phone. You may want to purchase CheckMate, a kit that can detect traces of semen that linger for many hours after sex. The company selling the kit suggests you test creatively; don't just go for underwear, try towels and socks. Love Detector is a "simple, friendly service" that analyzes how your partner feels about you by using voice-analysis technology. You call the Love Detector number and then your rat of a partner who has no idea there is also some voice-analysis technology on the line. When the chat is over the company provides an in-depth analysis on how embarrassed she was. What it won't tell you is if she's having sex with that guy you're worried about.

The more traditional route—rifling through her things (for example, credit-card statements or a diary), watching for suspicious computer or cell phone behavior, and sniffing for the smell of someone else's aftershave—is cheaper. Even more cost effective is the approach quoted by Menstuff.org, which says that instinct accurately detects infidelity for 85 percent of men and 50 percent of women. The figure is un-substantiated, but that gut-wrenching feeling you get when the person you're with is somehow different is very real. Infidelity can make people intensely angry as well as sad.

It's also quite common. In the *Handbook of Divorce and Romantic Relationship Dissolution*, researchers Julie H. Hall and Frank D. Fincham write that over two-thirds of the college students they spoke with reported being unfaithful; studies usually come up with figures for married couples that range from 25 to up to 60 percent of men and 40 percent of women. (There is a wide variation in the surveys and studies, as how they are done determines how honest people are.) Researchers used to think men had affairs for the sex and women for the love they were missing at home. Now that we all know women enjoy sex too, they think it's mostly just about getting more sex, for both men and women. Many affairs do start at work. The research organization One Plus One says that women are three times as likely to have an affair if they work away from home, even if they travel infrequently. An Australian study of 119 people (between the ages of seventeen and twenty-five) found that affairs among couples who were dating were more likely to happen when there were attractive people around to be unfaithful with and when the relationship was not very happy. Both of which are sufficiently shallow reasons to be a worry.

You may get proof and decide to challenge your girl-friend, or you may let events unfold. An MSNBC.com survey of 70,288 people found that most affairs ended within six months. If you ask her point-blank, she may lie or, worse, ac-cuse you of paranoia. The MSNBC survey found about 50 per-cent of both sexes had cheated but only 6 percent admitted it on direct questioning (although the number of people who were asked is not given). You may want to improve your rela-tionship anyway. Tell your girlfriend how much she means to you (if it's not much, her infidelity is less of a blow), go out together, call her at work to say hi (but don't say, "Hi, are you sitting on X's lap?"), be interested in what she is doing (but don't scare her). If you do find out she is having an affair, that's actually the easy bit. It's far harder to make your rela-tionship work afterward.

Me or the Missus?

> I'm in love with a man who is married with two children. I met him through work and we became friends, but for two years we've been lovers. He hasn't been close to his wife for years and says he won't stay in an unhappy marriage once the chil-dren are older. But, realistically (and selfishly), is there any chance he'll leave her for me?

Will your lover and father of two leave his wife for you? You'd be hard-pressed to find anyone who'd encourage you to hang around to find out. Not because it's morally wrong to have an affair with a married father of two (not ideal behavior though, is it?) but because the odds are not in your favor. There aren't many numbers, but those that exist make grim reading.

I could only find studies published in books, not in peer-reviewed psychology journals. There's a much quoted study by the psychologist Dr. Jan Halper, reported in her book *Quiet Desperation—The Truth about Successful Men*. Halper interviewed 4,126 "successful" male business leaders and executives. She found that 88 percent of them were equally successful in the bedroom as the boardroom, having had at least one affair. But she found that only 3 percent of those men left their wife for the woman they were having an affair with. Dr. Lana Staheli, in her book *Affair-Proof Your Marriage*, claims that less than 10 percent of people divorce their spouses to marry their lovers, and when they do, up to 70 percent of these marriages also end in divorce. An even more pessimistic failure rate of 75 percent is quoted by the psychiatrist Frank Pittman in his book *Private Lies: Infidelity and the Betrayal of Intimacy*, which is based on interviews with one hundred adulterous couples (his term, not mine). Pittman says these marriages don't work out because reality bites (everyday living together is not as glamorous as snatched hotel sex), there's too much guilt, or the person who initiated the affair is not trusted not to do so again. As the saying goes, when a man marries his mistress, he creates a job vacancy.

This is not to say your man is leading you on—only that he may be. Ruth Houston, an infidelity expert who set up infidelityadvice.com, has interviewed around ten thousand cheaters and cheatees (as she calls them) over thirteen years. She says that most men who have affairs aren't unhappy in their relationships; they mostly do it for the sex or the boost to their egos. She agrees with other researchers that they don't want to leave their wives. Her own research (which started when she discovered her husband, now her ex, was

having an affair) finds that if the wives find out and the husbands do leave, the men usually want to start afresh. Completely afresh.

Of course, you may have a different experience. The
problem with asking, "Will he leave her for me?" is that it's the
wrong question. "Should I get out and start seeing someone
else?" is a better one, with the more optimistic answer: yes.

Too Many Cooks

> After several failed monogamous relationships, my
> partner believes that, for him, open polyamory is a
> more honest and natural way to accommodate lov-
> ing more than one person. Is there any evidence
> that such relationships can work satisfactorily, and
> might they even work better than secretive relation-
> ships, which are common and cause vast numbers
> of broken monogamous relationships?

"Polyamory" means having more than one relationship at the
same time with the knowledge and consent of all partners
involved. Love is meant to be involved, which distinguishes it
from swinging. Polys, as they are known, aim to have sex
within another loving relationship and not just to throw their
car keys into a bowl in some stranger's living room. Polys argue that monogamy is dishonest and unnatural (no wonder,
they argue, that infidelity is rife). What little research there is
shows that for polyamory to work, you both have to want it.
But there's more: couples have to be able to communicate
well, respect each other, and agree that their relationship is
the "primary" one, which should be preserved. You also need
to be a stranger to jealousy or possessiveness (both much

more common than infidelity). If your relationship is this strong, you would think it could survive monogamy.

Some polys live in communities and share the fridge and child care, but most don't. Since they don't all wear badges saying "I'm a poly," it is hard to identify them and undertake research on their lifestyle. Estimates of the popularity of polyamory are likely to be wildly inaccurate. In the United States, enthusiasts estimate there are half a million polys, but acknowledge that many of them won't know what polyamory is and will think they are just having sex with other people from time to time. Polyamory is more common among male couples; polyamorists (but no one else) estimate that one-third of all male couples are polys.

There isn't any convincing evidence to suggest that polys are any happier than monogamous couples. A study in the *Journal of Family and Economic Issues* of 150 Dutch couples in open marriages (these were not defined as polyamorous but seemed to have similar rules) showed that they were just as happy and well adjusted as monogamous couples—not that they were more so. Since no one needs to sneak off to have an affair, are these relationships more enduring than monogamous ones?

Poly supporters often cite a study by Elaine Cook in the *Electronic Journal of Human Sexuality* that, they claim, shows that poly relationships last at least as long as monogamous ones. But the study only followed seven couples who had been together for five years, and Cook is a poly who was friends with four of the couples. Her conclusions—that polyamory works because despite other choices people stay in their primary relationship out of love and a "connection"—are therefore not reliable. Sorry. There are other studies; one in the *Family Coordinator* in 1975 that analyzed 380 people who had been in open relationships for ten years showed that they were happy and that their relationship with their partner had improved. But there was no comparison group and no studies of people who drop out of polyamory.

There are lots of poly fans, but most people stick with monogamy. A study of over 33,500 people in twenty-four countries published in the *Journal of Sex Research* found that 85 percent disapproved of extramarital sex. If you can deal with social disapproval on a global scale, that's great. Just make sure you don't become a poly to keep your partner, as there's no evidence it will do that.

Green-eyed Monster

> I have a lovely boyfriend who I think is gorgeous, but when he talks to other women at parties I feel jealous, and when he goes out after work I get all tortured imagining him flirting with other women. I've got no reason to think he would be unfaithful, and he always reassures me. My jealousy is irritating him now—how can I stop it?

Jealousy is so painful and widespread that you'd have to suspect it exists for a reason. Poets, such as John Keats, have often suffered terribly from it (he always suspected his beloved Fanny Brawne was out partying with men while he was lying on his sickbed, though she wasn't), so it may serve a creative purpose. Evolutionary psychologists say that jealousy is an evolved behavior that kicks in when there's a threat to reproductive resources (that would be your boyfriend). Making sure that no one else is after your boyfriend ("mate guarding," as it's called) may be especially strong for women around the time of ovulation. The threat may be real or imagined, although it's unclear why mate guarding has to make you feel sick to the pit of your stomach or want to mutilate your significant other's clothes. But then evolution is an imperfect process.

Women are traditionally threatened by attractive rivals, men by rivals who earn more than they do. At the heart of jealousy is the fear that you've lost control over someone else's feelings—that they've gone off and had feelings for, or just a good time with, someone else. But studies do find that some people are unhealthily jealous of their mate's hobbies or families, anything that takes time away from them.

Much of the research asks people how jealous they would feel about hypothetical events, so it is not that reliable. A questionnaire survey of 132 people by the University of Wisconsin, Madison, looked at the connection between uncertainty in relationships and jealousy. It found that people in less certain relationships were most jealous about anyone they thought their partner might want to have sex with. More secure couples felt most jealous about their partner becoming emotionally close to someone else. They found that personal insecurity didn't make people more jealous, so it's not some self-worth problem you need to deal with.

You should ask yourself what you're worried about. Is it that someone else is enjoying his company, or is it that you'll lose him? Other studies show that jealousy can be corrosive to relationships. If you plan on an interrogation, you'll drive yourself bonkers and drive him as far away as possible. You need to remember not only that he's with you and no one else, but that he seems to want to avoid making you jealous. How committed is that?

Do your best to minimize your jealousy, but be aware that in small amounts it can spice up a relationship. A study of 226 people in the journal *Communication Reports* found that jealousy wasn't always negative; couples could laugh about it and find it a positive thing that their partner thought them desirable to other people. A jealous episode can even make sex more passionate. Try to deal with your jealousy by using humor and honesty rather than by distancing yourself or getting upset. It doesn't sound like there's cause for jealousy. For now at least, you sound more irritated by your jealous feelings than he is.

Flirt Alert

> My boyfriend is always flirting with other women. He has a reputation for being a flirt, and I always hope there won't be an attractive woman when we go out because he'll talk to her and ignore me. He also gets flirty text messages. Should I just accept that's who he is and not get jealous, or can I make him stop?

Flirting, says a report from the Social Issues Research Study in Oxford, "is the foundation of civilization." Okay, so the report was funded by Martini (a company that sells liquor) and there were no references, but you can see that flirting could be essential to the survival of the human species. But what's wrong with your boyfriend flirting only with you?

To accuse someone of flirting, you must think there is some sexual intent. Otherwise that individual would just be good at talking to women (or men). There are moves in flirting that overlap with those of good conversationalists: listening intently, making eye contact, and touching to make a point (an arm, not a thigh). Other techniques such as eyebrow flashing (as in "I really know you, don't I?"), saying "You look gorgeous in that," leaning toward someone and looking at her cleavage (it happens) are 100 percent flirtatious. Flirtatious speech is more animated; flirts like to laugh and to look at the mouth of the person they're flirting with. Flirting can be, and often is, harmless and enjoyable, and is arguably an essential life skill.

That said, although a survey by *Men's Health* of 1,500 men found that 94 percent of men did not consider flirting to be unfaithful, this doesn't excuse men for doing it when their girlfriend is present. Over two-thirds of men said they would be flattered rather than jealous if a gorgeous man flirted with their girlfriend. Oh, really?

But there are some fine lines. The same proportion said that suggestive comments and flirty e-mails were fine, but kissing, unsurprisingly, was not. An international study, published in the *Journal of Sex Research,* of 877 male and 1,194 female students from countries ranging from the United States to Mexico and Hungary found that hugging or dancing with someone else did not make partners jealous, whereas flirting did. Even when romantic partners discussed sexual fantasies, it did not create the jealousy that flirting did. And it may bother women more than men.

A study in *Personal Relationships* following 219 college students also showed that more women than men considered flirting to be unfaithful. This does not mean they don't do it themselves. The MSNBC.com survey of 70,288 people found that 53 percent of men and 73 percent of women thought sending a sexually flirtatious e-mail counted as cheating.

Flirting, as you've found, is also done via cell phones (although only 8 percent of people flirt this way, according to a YouGov survey of over five thousand people in the United Kingdom) and through social-networking sites such as Facebook. The distance and unreality of the medium can make messages become rapidly more explicit.

Even if your boyfriend is an innocent flirt, he could tone it down a bit. You could ask him why he flirts. Is he insecure (use another term of course), does he want a response from you, does he even know how horrible it makes you feel? He probably doesn't take the flirting further, but that doesn't mean you should accept it. If you can't make him stop flirting, at least watch how he does it and pick up some useful tips for finding your next boyfriend.

Truth or Dare?

> I had a short affair with a woman I used to work with (we did a stressful project together). I really regret it, but I don't know whether to tell my wife about my affair or not. Is there a "good" way to tell her?

It's a case of being damned if you do tell and damned if you don't. On balance, you may do more damage to your relationship by not telling her, but the evidence for this is too flimsy to be reliable. Infidelity is unpopular with everyone; surveys show that over 80 to 90 percent of people think it's wrong, largely for moral reasons. Yet people still do it. The General Social Survey, based at the University of Chicago, uses a national sample to track how Americans behave. The survey data show that each year about 12 percent of married men and 7 percent of married women admit to having been unfaithful. Data cited by the Kinsey Institute (from an older, smaller study) show that 94 percent of married men and women had only one sex partner (their spouse) in the past twelve months, while 4 percent had two to four partners and 1 percent had five or more partners. Rates are higher in casual relationships.

Most people in committed relationships attempt (even halfheartedly) to stay together after an affair. How someone finds out about the affair does seem to make a difference, but it's not clear how much this influences the eventual outcome. A study of 105 college students (men and women) in the *Journal of Social and Personal Relationships* shows that when the person admitted (unasked) to an affair, 56 percent of couples stayed together, compared to 14 percent when the partner found out on direct questioning. Having to ask and then being told confers a double whammy; your partner not only cheated but lied (through omission) about it first. Relationships do recover from infidelity, and being married improves your chances of survival. Being miserably married for years, or having an affair to get back at your partner, however, does not.

There's no "good" way to tell your wife, only a "less bad" way. This is a grim business. Your wife will be angry, but worse for your relationship, she will torture herself by running through the gory details in her mind and wondering what's so wrong with her that you had to have sex with someone else. She will believe she can no longer trust you.

There are no data on what will happen if you don't tell her or on the chances of her finding out anyway. But studies on secrets in relationships show it requires a huge effort not to blurt them out, and concentrating in order to keep your mouth shut can create distance between you. But then divorce creates distance too.

Telling her yourself gives you some control over how she finds out. You can give a consistent story, making sure you sound incredibly sorry and explain why you cheated—cite circumstances rather than blaming your wife. Promise both to never do it again and to do your best to make it right. Once the horror has faded, you can try repairing and improving your relationship, but don't expect instant forgiveness. That lightness of spirit you may have after telling her about your affair will be at her expense. She'll be the one who's now burdened with this knowledge.

Complete honesty is not the best policy, though, so stick to essential facts. Don't ever be drawn into details such as what the other woman looked like or what sex toys you used, the luxury hotels you used them in—obvious stuff, perhaps. Even worse would be a frank discussion on how much you felt for the woman you had the affair with (unless it was very little). There's only so much disclosure a relationship can take, however well it's done.

Just Good Friends

> My boyfriend has a close female friend from his last job whom he sees without me. I don't really like it, and my friends think I'm stupid to let him see her. Most men I've been out with started out as "just friends." Should I trust him, or is it naive to think he's only friends with her?

The "Can men and women just be friends?" question is rather complicated. Surveys show that many romantic relationships start off as friendships (over half), but this may be because one person is attracted to the other and chooses a let's-be-pals rather than a direct approach. A poll on the women's Web site handbag.com found overwhelming support (83 percent of the 1,811 votes cast) for the idea of men and women being able to be platonic friends. But, oops, nearly half of the women said some male friends were ex-lovers, and one-third of the women secretly lusted after their male friends but didn't act on it because of the risk to their friendship. Men are more likely to be attracted to their women friends than vice versa; a survey by MarketTiers of one thousand Americans found that one-third of men have a crush on one of their close female friends.

Some psychologists believe cross-sex relationships really can be platonic because of the phenomenon of friendship attraction. People value the same characteristics in friends as they do in lovers, but there's more of an emphasis on lust and physical attraction in romantic relationships. In platonic friendships any physical attraction has to be ignored or at least not acted upon. Friendships that work are highly valued, with men saying they enjoy talking to someone about things other than sports and women feeling they get to understand men a bit more.

Yet these relationships are potentially more complicated than same-sex friendships. Vickie Harvey, a researcher from California State University, was driven to study them because of her intense friendships with some male work colleagues. She asked 120 college students to keep a journal for sixteen weeks, each discussing one platonic friendship. She found that while some friendships start out as testing grounds for relationships, that moment usually passes. However, at some stage a quarter of these friends had kissed or held hands, although generally the relationship quickly shifted back to being platonic. Most of the students wanted to keep their friendship platonic even if they felt attracted to each other.

So your boyfriend probably is just friends with this woman, and you can trust him because he's chosen to go out with you. Some men are more able than others to be friends with women, and you'll have a good idea of whether your boyfriend is one of them—especially if you invite yourself along one evening. He would be smart to introduce you to her (and if he doesn't, you should push for it), since if you get to know her you're likely to be less concerned about their relationship. In the meantime watch out for warning phrases of growing intimacy, such as, "I told X all about our fight in the car/having sex in the garden." No one likes a cross-sex friend knowing personal stuff about their relationship. You may want to take some preventative measures to protect your relationship, like asking him specific questions about his work and interests and how he feels about things—both trivial and profound. Make sure you have time together and go out and have fun. Basically be a pal to him yourself.

Break-ups or Make-ups?

Revenge Is Sour

> My boyfriend has always flirted in front of me and made it clear he's interested in other women, and now he's dumped me for someone he works with. I'm so angry that all I can think of is how to get back at him and hurt him. Would taking some revenge make me feel better, and if so, what should I do?

You're clear on why you want revenge (and well-defined goals are good), but any idea that you'll feel better afterward may be misguided. However, it's worth reviewing the common methods of revenge for women, which include calling expensive sex lines from his phone and leaving the phone off the hook, burning clothes (his), telling work colleagues and friends he's a coke fiend (assuming he isn't), and having sex with his best friend. Posting intimate videos online is usually a man's thing.

In a study of eighty-eight Canadians by researchers at the University of Calgary, the most popular methods of revenge were flirting with friends or enemies of their ex, keying their ex's car, breaking something their former partner loved (excluding the ex's arms or legs), writing nasty notes to their ex, and gossiping (with a megaphone) about how useless their ex was in bed. The most popular revenge method for people still with the partner they're angry with was either flirting in front of the partner or the silent treatment (not much use if you're no longer together).

So pick your revenge weapon of choice by all means, but will it make you feel better? In trying to get even, you probably want your ex to feel hurt and humiliated. Ideally, even more than you do. A study by Stephen Yoshimura at the University of Montana asked 152 people (average age twenty) what acts of revenge they had carried out, what they had wanted to achieve by them, and how they felt afterward. He found that most people who'd spread rumors about their ex, taken their ex's stuff, or damaged their ex's property felt anxious and sorry rather than joyful afterward. But most of all, they still felt angry. People wanted their revenge to punish their ex and to make themselves feel more in control. But taking revenge only seemed to make them feel marginally better and in the end rather more thoroughly miserable. It's hard to do things you'd normally think are wrong—even when you're doing them to a complete jerk. Unfortunately, for most people, revenge is not a jolly act of retribution.

So why not try the traditional ways of making yourself feel sexy and therefore making your ex regret his actions? For example, you could starve yourself to a size zero or buy some breast implants. (I'm kidding.) However angry you are now, the odds are you'll be just as angry if you take revenge. Just as you'd be more hurt if you were still with him than without him. It sounds like you're well rid of him. You'll feel much better if you send him a thank-you card instead.

Post-Traumatic Love Disorder

> Is there such a thing as post-traumatic love syndrome? If there isn't, there should be. I broke up with my girlfriend three years ago after a stormy relationship and haven't seen her since, but I can't stop thinking about her and missing her badly every day. What is wrong with me?

The break-up of a relationship can be one of life's most traumatic events. Many studies document the depression and heart disease (it would be heart disease) that occur in some people after divorce. However, it's not only divorce that can wreak havoc on one's physical and emotional well-being. A Canadian study of 5,254 women and 4,521 men between the ages of twenty and sixty-four, published in the *Journal of Marriage and Family*, found the same effects for people who split up after living together (a rise in depression and decline in physical health, in this study felt more by men). The break-up of any strongly felt relationship can be intensely traumatic.

There probably should be such a thing as post-traumatic love syndrome. It would have to be considered as a lesser condition than post-traumatic stress disorder (PTSD), because it doesn't involve a life-threatening incident such as an act of terrorism (being a hostage of love doesn't count) or plane crash, but it may share symptoms. These include reliving the moment, avoidance and emotional numbing (you avoid places and people who remind you of what happened), and being hypervigilant in case it happens again.

119

In less psychiatric and more everyday terms, you'll be less open, more irritable, and anxious. You may feel distant from other people and less interested in just about everything. Being traumatized after any event is linked to feeling helpless about what happened during the event itself; so you may feel you couldn't change things even if you wanted to. Did you initiate the split? Researchers at the University of Colorado performed a study of 144 newly separated husbands and wives and found that people who didn't initiate the split were likely to suffer more afterward, feeling out of control and more distressed. It didn't seem to matter how unhappy their relationships were beforehand; they suffered just the same. You feel that you had little or no control over the relationship break-up, but your ex-girlfriend probably felt the same way.

Just as people with PTSD are more likely to get depressed and develop drug and alcohol problems, so are divorced men. Has this happened to you? Three years to get over your girl-friend is not pathological, but it isn't healthy. Getting over this event requires reorganization—of your thoughts and your life. You should talk it through with someone you can trust. If this doesn't help, you need to train yourself to think about it differently. Most important, you need to be less preoccupied by thoughts of your ex. Over 75 percent of people with PTSD recover with time, and now that you've had time, you should consider some treatments. Those that may work for a trauma-tized lover include relaxation therapy, cognitive therapy (talking to a therapist can help you to look at things differently), and eye-movement treatments that desensitize you to the trauma. Traditional psychotherapy is a larger investment that could take another three years. Many people do think about their exes every day. You'll know you're over her when you think about her and it doesn't hurt.

> For the last three years I've gone out with friends to some great New Year's Eve parties. Then around midnight I'm suddenly overwhelmed by thinking about my ex-boyfriend whom I split up with three years ago. I lived with him for nearly four years, and although I feel I'm over him, at this time each year it's like the break-up happened yesterday. It's so embarrassing—usually I start crying really loudly in the kitchen. Why does this loss still hit me so hard, and will the pain ever get better?

Why, I wonder, do you cry really loudly instead of stuffing tissues into your mouth to keep the noise down? After three years of audible sobbing, you must have very good friends to still get invited out.

Alcohol, the countdown to the new year, and "Auld Lang Syne" are failproof catalysts for nostalgic longing. New Year's Eve can be a good excuse for crying about any loss; a mourning of the old as much as a celebration of the new. And if thoughts about your ex are to pop up at any time, it's at "Happy New Year!" time when you start asking yourself: "So how happy am I?" "Wasn't I happier with X?" "What's X doing right now?"

I'm not unsympathetic. According to some often quoted research—unfortunately, I haven't been able to find the original paper—one needs an average of one month per year of a relationship to get over someone. Other research into marriages that break up suggests it takes a year and half for people to start feeling happy again.

If you aren't romantically involved with anyone yet, the

121

odds are that you soon will be. But nothing can really insure you against memories on New Year's Eve. Should you block out upsetting thoughts about ex-lovers? The studies are fairly primitive, and the results are inconclusive. One study from the University of Virginia measured electrical impulses across the skin of seventy young people, and found that suppressing thoughts of ex-lovers (when the person was still sad about them) increased stress and anxiety levels. Some neuroscientists from the University of South Carolina got excited when they found that by measuring brain activity in eleven women who were mourning the loss of recent relationships, they were able to pinpoint the exact parts of the brain that felt grief. So brain surgery could help. Again, I'm just kidding.

Many studies show that you are more likely to get over someone if you initiated the split, have a career to keep you busy, have a large social network of friends to tell you that you can do better, and, to a lesser extent, if you have a new lover. New relationships generally do help, though on New Year's Eve there's the risk that a few drinks and a dollop of selective memories can make any current mate seem less desirable than a former flame. Psychologists have published reams on the attachment theory of relationships, saying that relationships create a strong biological bond that causes physical and emotional distress at separation. Some people, perhaps you, are predisposed to react more strongly to the loss of a relationship. This may be because you got so attached that you're still struggling to let go. He is not your mom or dad, so it's okay to forget about him.

Please don't cry this year. If your ex pops into your head, shove him back out again or concentrate on his bad points. Otherwise your sobbing will upset people who don't know you, and, worse, when the clock chimes twelve, no one will want to give you a new year's kiss.

Unfair Affair

> I had a brief relationship with a woman who was the friend of a work colleague. She ended it because it "wasn't going anywhere." I was devastated because I felt I was falling in love with her, and now I can't stop thinking about her. It's been a month now, and sometimes I drive past her house on purpose and feel like a stalker. How could I have got it so wrong, and how can I get over her?

Unrequited love is nearly a universal experience. It is the stuff of literature—Cyrano de Bergerac had it badly but carried it nobly, and Jane Austen's heroines were highly susceptible—but things usually worked out in the end. In real life, where unrequited love usually stays that way, it causes deep despair. A study of 155 men and women by researchers at Case Western Reserve University in Ohio, published in the *Journal of Personality and Social Psychology*, found that only 2 percent of the subjects had never experienced unrequited love (defined as an intense, passionate yearning that is not reciprocated). The study counted both being rejected by and rejecting someone as an "experience." Men were a third more likely than women to have suffered unrequited love. Those who did the rejecting felt guilty (claiming overall to feel worse than those they rejected) but also irritated by any attempts by the rejected to win them back.

Some people are more prone to unrequited love than others, so you want to be careful, even in the midst of your grief, not to make it a habit. It may sound obvious, but if you are anxious about relationships, emotionally needy, and fall in love at the drop of a hat, the main thing you're courting is disappointment. Passion is great, but too much, too soon, can push people away; a little restraint is not just attractive, but essential for self-preservation. A recent study, published in the *Journal of Social and Personal Relationships*, asked over three hundred men and women to report their experiences of falling in love; the researchers found that this blissful state was triggered not only by the desirability of the other person but also by the confidence that the loving feeling was mutual. Most people fall in love with someone they are pretty sure loves them back. Falling in love just works better that way. It is possible to misread someone else's signals, and other studies show that rejected lovers often feel they were "led on." But if you keep getting it wrong, it's you and not them who needs a talking-to.

It's also possible for long-term relationships to end with one person still in love with the other. This scenario is more painful, and often the announcement comes out of the blue. But in a short-lived relationship you should be able to move on relatively painlessly. Loving-and-losing is romantic, but stalking is obsessive. Stop now. Grieve for another week maximum, then get out there, keep busy, try again, and tell yourself that everyone loses in love sometimes. No one wants to dent your enthusiasm for love, but it's an activity in which receiving is as important as giving.

Cuddling Deficiency

I have been with my man for almost four years, and we love each other deeply. Unfortunately, he struggles with demonstrating his feelings. His lack of affection makes me feel lonely and unattractive. He says he doesn't need affection, although he cuddles

> me during sleep. He is unable to relax during love-making and behaves like an embarrassed teenager in bed. How can I make him see that I am a woman who needs a smattering of affection and the odd compliment?

Your man is not comfortable with intimacy, and it gets worse the more intimate you get. But he sounds like a nice guy; perhaps the cuddling in bed redeems him. You also seem confident that he loves you, and that confidence must derive from something he says or does. He must behave as though he loves you. His problems with demonstrating his feelings, at least physically, are nothing personal, so it's a shame you're feeling lonely and unattractive.

Might you feel better if you knew that women are generally more "touchy-feely" in relationships than men? The evidence, however, isn't clear. A study in the *Journal of Social and Personal Relationships* had researchers select 154 couples waiting in lines outside movie theaters and observe how often they touched within a two-minute period. They then went up to the couples and asked them how long they'd been together. They found there were no differences between how often men and women started touching their romantic partner, and, as you might expect, longer-term couples were less likely to touch each other. But this didn't mean they weren't close. The longer-term couples rated themselves closer than other couples; they just didn't show as much affection to each other. At least not while in line. The researchers didn't follow them home.

Intimacy is important in relationships because when reciprocated it makes people feel good about themselves and confident and committed in their relationships. You feel lonely because you want that closeness. Researchers at the

125

University of Nevada asked 248 people what they did to show commitment to their partner. The behavior that came out on top? Providing affection, such as hugs and kisses, and saying "I love you." Women in this study said they gave more affection than men did, but the difference was barely significant. Compliments weren't mentioned, although fidelity as a way of showing commitment was highly popular. Other studies show the importance of talking to each other openly about how you feel about things. If you can't talk to each other, that would be more worrying than his inability to hug.

There's evidence that the more affectionate you are, the more it's reciprocated, so don't give up. Keep cuddling and snuggling up—start on the sofa and don't make any sudden moves. You need to take the lead in a noncritical way and explain how you feel about him as a lover and what you need in a relationship. Let him know that although you love him, you're lonely. Don't be critical, but do be clear about what you're asking him to do. You may need to look at getting some professional help with the sex, although many books provide exercises to help relaxation and responsiveness in bed. Perhaps you wish you'd met someone as affectionate as you are but you haven't, so you can either leave this man you love or try again to encourage him to be more affectionate.

Alpha Male Alert

I've been in a long-distance relationship for a year and a half with a guy I really admire. He's intelligent and attractive, but he's such an alpha male! I love chatting; I'm into the arts. But he's an engineer who cares more about watching sports than talking to me. Obviously he's never said one word about his

> emotions; he snaps that he's "not a girl," and, though I sense that he cares for me, he's never said anything to that effect. The solution is probably to move on and find a guy who really communicates. Is there any hope?

There should always be hope, whatever disaster you're facing, but more than hope, you want a chat. Now, to many women, alpha males are very attractive, even when they are engineers. These men are dominant (as are the alpha males in animal groups) and have the pick of womankind. Women, however, are generally sensible enough to look for other attributes in long-term relationships, such as compassion, support, intimacy, love, and security, according to most research. For example, a study published in the *Journal of Personality and Social Psychology* asked 751 college students for the qualities they most wanted in mates. Attributes such as being hostile and dismissive (as in barking "I'm not a girl!") did not rate highly. The study showed that people are attracted to others who share their attitudes, but what made for happy relationships were similar personality traits. If you are a chatty extrovert and he won't talk, the odds are probably against you. If you want intimacy and he doesn't, you're both going to get upset. In this age of emotional incontinence, refusing to emote can seem rather refreshing. But not when you're trying to establish some basic level of intimacy.

If you are fundamentally different, maybe there is less optimism than you might be hoping for. A study in the *Proceedings of the National Academy of Sciences* asked 978 men and women (ages eighteen to twenty-four) to rate ten attributes in a mate and then rank the same attributes as they applied to themselves. These attributes included wealth, family commitment, and fidelity. When people thought an attribute especially

127

important in a mate, they put it at the top of their list when ranking their own attributes. The study was a "what if" rather than a real-life trial, but it suggests that people pick people who are like them.

Some people deliberately avoid intimacy because they don't want to need other people or because they are afraid to. They may choose partners who are like them and from whom they can keep a safe distance. There are many research papers linking intimacy avoidance to insecure relationships in childhood. You can't psychoanalyze your guy's early relationships, but you can let him know you won't reject him should he choose to tell you how he feels. Having a supportive relationship (that includes sex) with someone has been shown to improve people's mental and physical health and can right some of the wrongs experienced in childhood. Despite what he says, he's likely to be happier if he talks like a girl sometimes.

You ask if your man can become less of an alpha male. Will he change? He may if he wants to, but should you even try? Other men can and do talk and will even say "I love you" from time to time. Your guy may care for you, but you're saying that's not enough. Put in a concerted effort, and if it fails, consider increasing the length of your long distance.

Gone for Good?

I've been living with my boyfriend for two years, but he's in a band and often away. He's said he wants some space to see how he feels about the relationship. He's taken some of his things. But on the phone he says he misses me. Is he likely to come back?

Do you want him back? It sounds like he's forgotten that a relationship involves two people and has made a unilateral decision about what he wants. You must be wondering what that space he wants looks like. Is it in his head or some other woman's bed?

I imagine you're hoping he'll have a change of heart, but the research suggests most break-ups are for good. A study in the *Journal of Marriage and Family* in 2003 found that only a third of relationships that break up get back together, and those that do tend to be the more established ones, with children and shared mortgages. If you are under thirty, the long-term reconciliation rate is one in ten.

No one can predict what will happen to you—these are just the odds found in various studies, some of which were carried out on university students (you may be older and thus the results are less applicable)—but the statistics are probably starker than you'd expect. Why shouldn't your ex change his mind? He says he misses you, and he hasn't changed his phone number. Unfortunately, the evidence is that leaving is less a physical and more an emotional act. When someone leaves, they've usually wanted to do so for months. Nobody wakes up one morning and suddenly decides, "I want out."

Research published in the *Journal of Personality and Social Psychology* from the University of Texas shows a clear pattern in the death of a relationship. Your boyfriend will have thought about how much he gets out of the relationship, if it has a future, and, I'm sorry to say, how easy it will be to find someone else. He will have rehearsed his arguments for leaving you in his head and with his friends. By downplaying his uncertainty when he talks to you, he makes it easy to leave while keeping a foot in the door in case he changes his mind or wants to have sex with you again.

So if you are in the majority of couples who don't get back together, you will need to get over him. The mess and sadness of breaking up is not a terminal condition. The research shows that once you know he's gone for good, you'll be less upset.

There is no clear evidence on how long it takes to get over someone. Some psychologists say it's a month for every year you've been together. Most of us will know people who seem to recover much faster. Your boyfriend will have been at least a few months ahead of you in deciding it was over; now you need to catch up.

If you wonder if he's hurting as much as you—he isn't. Even if he says "I feel terrible," he doesn't feel as bad as you do. The Texas study shows that the person who didn't initiate the break-up feels worse because they didn't have a choice in the matter. But that's not to say that in six months you won't be the happier one.

Gullible or Gutted?

My husband came home from a business trip two months ago and told me he's gay. We've been married quite happily for five years, always had sex, so I was devastated when he told me. We're getting divorced—quite amicably (and I had a negative HIV test which reassured me). But I'm sure my friends don't believe me when I say I didn't know. Am I stupid not to have noticed anything?

Most women whose husbands come out have no idea they are gay. Much of the research in this area has been carried out by Amity Pierce Buxton, whose husband came out as gay after twenty-five years of marriage. Buxton, who lives in San Francisco, realized there wasn't much support (her friends were embarrassed, and so was she), so she set up the Straight Spouse Network. It now has over sixty-five branches worldwide. She's the world expert, having interviewed eleven thousand gay and straight spouses and published her research in a book, *The Other Side of the Closet*, and in academic journals such as the *Journal of Homosexuality*.

Her research shows that most women, like you, are shattered when their husbands tell them they're gay. If you haven't already, you'll go through a painful grieving process, feeling deceived, angry, and shocked before accepting you've lost the mate and future you thought you had. Buxton found that while some women think infidelity in such situations feels worse because it's with a man, others feel better because there's nothing they could have done about it. In Buxton's surveys one-third of couples divorce right away, another third break up after a year, and the rest stay together, usually in open marriages.

Your friends are wrong if they think you must have known. A study in the *Journal of Homosexuality* of twenty-one women married to homosexual or bisexual men, carried out by the University of Pennsylvania, found that only five suspected their husband might be attracted to men. This was a small study (it's not easy to find women in this situation) but a useful one because it asked women in detail what their relationships had been like. Most said they'd had good sex lives and had happy marriages. And although many felt, looking back, their husbands had become distant and gone off sex over the years, they suspected affairs with other women—not men. There were no pink neon signs; other research shows that gay married men can be actively homophobic in an attempt to hide their sexuality. All of the women felt anger and grief that were made worse by feeling deceived and stupid for not guessing the truth. Most found out by their husbands telling them directly.

You might want to ask your husband why he married you. Buxton's research shows that even now some gay men marry women because they want a family life and children. They may also fall intellectually in love with a woman while wanting sex with men. Many couples in your situation stay friends because this companionable love remains.

Buxton estimates that 1 to 2 percent of marriages have one gay spouse. This is backed up by older studies (such as one in the *Social Problems Journal*) that find similar rates across Europe. So it isn't uncommon, and you're not stupid—it's a devastating revelation.

In the Genes?

> My girlfriend and I are thinking of getting married. We've been together for five years, and I'd like us to get married before we have kids. My parents have been happily married for thirty years. But her parents got divorced when she was twelve, and she's worried this makes it more likely that we'll get divorced. Does it?

I hate to say this, but your girlfriend's right. The research is clear that if you have divorced parents, this increases your own chances of getting divorced. Risk factors can often be hard to quantify—but sadly not in this case. A large U.S. study conducted over the course of twenty years involving more than two thousand people found that the chances of a couple getting divorced increased by nearly 70 percent if the wife's parents had split up. If the parents of both the husband and wife divorced, their own risk of doing so increased by 190 percent. Other studies seem to confirm these results.

As you might expect, researchers have tried to figure out why divorce might be, as they say, "transmitted across generations." It's not just one generation either. There's a study by researchers at Pennsylvania State University of 691 families showing that divorce is more likely in couples whose grandparents got divorced. But these statistics are not the death knell for your marriage prospects. They can give you a forecast of the general risk but not your own specific risk. On the plus side, forewarned is forearmed.

You can probably guess the theories behind these patterns of divorce. (If not, ask your girlfriend about her parents' divorce.) The studies in the United States and in many other countries show that it's parental behavior that casts the shadow over the marriages of subsequent generations. The six key behaviors that mess up someone's grandparents', parents', and their own chances of marital bliss are being jealous, domineering, angry, critical, moody, and noncommunicative with a spouse. These behaviors upset a couple's children, who grow up without learning that partners should support each other and resolve issues in an amicable fashion. These studies do take into account how the children are parented; you can be a better parent than you are a spouse (though conflict in relationships doesn't do much for children). But it seems that children copy how their parents got along with each other, rather than how they were nurtured themselves. The children of parents who fought their way to the divorce courts grow up, not surprisingly, to be pessimistic about lifelong relationships and fairly enthusiastic about divorce once the honeymoon period is over. They are less likely to trust and commit to relationships. They will not have seen their parents get through the bad times or handle conflict in constructive ways. The divorce is actually incidental; the research suggests that it's the damage done beforehand that affects the adult relationships of the children involved.

Even amicable divorces increase the risk of children from these families getting divorced. It's not clear whether children who grow up with parents who are unhappy but don't split up have an increased risk of divorce, but they are more likely to have unhappy relationships themselves.

So back to you. There are many children of divorced parents who have strong marriages. Marital success is predicated on many things, not just your family history. Your girlfriend's reticence may be due to her suspicion that she has problems with trust and commitment, but you don't, and together you may have the resilience to have a long and happy marriage. And if it all goes downhill, you can always blame your in-laws.

Third Time Lucky?

> I am about to marry a lovely man who is everything my first husband wasn't. He talks to me, we do things with my children as a family, and we should have a great future together. The only thing I worry about is the fact that he's been married twice before (he has two children). Is he more likely to get divorced again, this time from me?

Does practice make perfect? Sadly no, if what you're practicing is marriage. Each year over 40 percent of weddings are remarriages, a doubling of the rate thirty years ago, according to One Plus One, a UK research organization for couples and families. Unfortunately, these remarriages may be a triumph of optimism over realism; nearly half of all second marriages fail, and nearly 60 percent of third marriages do, too. This does not mean that your marriage will not be a triumph, but statistically it is more likely to fail than your first marriage and his second one.

Why should this be? Research published in the *Journal of Marriage and Family* suggests that remarried spouses are quicker to criticize and get upset with their partners than those in first marriages. Most disagreements (and there are more than in first marriages) are about stepchildren—covering such often unsolvable problems as discipline, rules, and the amount of money spent on the kids. Remarried couples get along even worse when both parties have children because there is even more to argue about. "You treat your children differently from mine" is the signature tune of many reconstituted families. People who remarry may also be more impulsive and unrealistic about how relationships work, seeing divorce as a ready solution to any problem. Some people (well, most of us) not only fail to learn from their mistakes but also take them to their next relationship, where they once again cause trouble.

However, there is some evidence that remarriages are more equal when it comes to how decisions are made and how housework is distributed. According to a survey of nearly two thousand people by researchers at the University of Texas, despite the disagreements that seem to occur, remarriages that don't end quickly in divorce are almost as happy as first marriages (when the lengths of the marriages are compared).

So remarriages can be happy unions, and most research suggests that people who are married are better off emotionally and financially than those who are single or divorced (unless your marriage is chronically miserable). Most people who have divorced do go on to have further relationships in the expectation that they'll be happy. You seem to have found

135

someone who has qualities that you badly wanted and missed in your first marriage, which bodes well.

For the sake of yourself and your children, you need to make sure that your odds of success are as high as possible. If you haven't probed before, now's the time to do it. Discuss how you plan to bring up your children, in particular who will discipline them, and how. Ask your fiancé how you will resolve disputes together. Better still: although love is a wonderful thing, check if he's got any money—weddings are costly, but divorces and their aftermath are much more expensive.

7

Sex Lives

Tri-weekly

> I've been living with my girlfriend for about two
> years, and we get along really well. The problem is
> that we don't have much sex. When we first started
> going out, we had sex every day and it was great;
> now we can go days without it. Is this drop-off
> normal—does it happen to everyone?

What is it about sex that makes people worry if they're having
a "normal" amount? In most cases, including yours, there's no
need to worry. You and your girlfriend clearly used to have a
good sex life (assuming there was quality to go with quantity).
The problem is that nearly all couples have less sex the longer
they're together. Researchers partly blame a process called "ha-
bituation," a fancy way of saying that sex (with your long-term
partner) loses its novelty value. After the initial uncertainty

and excitement, the sex in your relationship may be pushed into the background by pressures at work, a tedious commute, or a long-running television series.

It's hard to benchmark your own sex life. Fortunately, it's been done for us. An early, famous survey, carried out by Alfred Kinsey in 1953, found that young married couples had sex a couple of times a week. In the 1990s, the National Health and Social Life Survey found married couples had sex around seven times a month, while the General Social Survey came up with just over once a week—though younger couples and those who had been together less than three years had more sex than that. Studies generally show the amount of sex a couple has starts to fall after a couple of years, whether they are still dating, living together, or married. So if you do go some days without sex, this really is normal. People under twenty-five have sex around twelve times a month, but even they have it less often the longer they've been in a relationship.

The average disguises a wide range—in most studies from no sex to forty-five times a month. The amount of sex you have as a couple is set by you, not by the national average, nor by what your friends are doing (should they tell you). A study by researchers from the Faculty of Arts and Sciences in New Brunswick, Canada, published in the *Journal of Sex Research*, found that in the first year couples develop a pattern for how often they have sex. And if they were above the average then, they will continue to be so, even after two years. So although mortgages and having kids are great contraceptives, a couple with both may still have more sex than the young child-free couple across the street—although it seems unlikely.

You may not have negotiated with your girlfriend just how much sex you want because it isn't a spontaneous and sexy thing to do. If you want more sex, there are numerous studies, as well as common sense, that say you should talk about it. You may have to make a conscious effort to set aside time for sex. The New Brunswick study found that taking turns to initiate sex made couples more satisfied with their sex lives, as did talking to each other about what they liked during sex. The study showed it's best to take a direct rather than euphemistic approach. Don't say, "Let's have an early night," because that's exactly what you'll get.

Try Weekly

> I've lost interest in sex. I really love my partner and have been with him for twelve years (we have two kids, who are eight and ten), but over the last year I've lost my sex drive. He's still attractive to me, but if he starts something it's a real effort for me to become aroused. I could probably do without sex altogether but know he couldn't. Is it normal to lose interest in sex? Would Viagra help me?

It's normal to lose interest in sex, but rather inconvenient if you're in a relationship. Many women say that once they've had children they go off sex (preferring sleep) or find it more challenging to get aroused. Surveys show that people do have sex when they don't want it, but when it becomes a huge effort this isn't an option. A study published in the *Journal of the American Medical Association* surveyed 1,749 women between the ages of eighteen and fifty-nine and found that 43 percent of them (compared with 31 percent of the 1,410 men surveyed) had problems with sex—mostly related to loss of desire and arousal. But this figure has been hotly debated as too high. Women were asked questions about lack of desire, anxiety about sexual performance, and difficulties with lubrication for two months or more. If they said yes to any one question, they were classified as having sexual problems. While pharmaceutical companies might like a woman's loss of interest in sex to be a medical problem, it really isn't a disease and it is not helpful to think of it as such. More realistically, a poll by London's *Observer* newspaper and ICM Research of 1,027 people found that only 19 percent said their sex drive was low or very low.

There are some medical reasons for losing interest in sex, including the pill, depression, alcohol, diabetes, anything that makes sex painful, menopause, quite a few medicines, and stress. But most often a change in desire is a reasonable response to the challenges of life. For example, a study at the National Institutes of Health found that women on low incomes were up to two-thirds more likely to have sexual problems than other women. Even without financial stress, many women find it hard to order their lives so that sex gets a time slot. In the long list of women's roles—mother, worker, friend, daughter—lover (unfortunately) comes last.

Desire and arousal have complex biological pathways that start in the brain. Viagra (which is not licensed for use by women) may get more blood to the genitals, but so does more foreplay and even the anticipation of foreplay. You have to do the cheesy stuff of making time for sex, avoiding the mundane (not in bed, legs up, with the lights out), and using music as a diversion to relieve inhibitions. You will need to masturbate more, use vibrators, massage, stimulate orally, and fantasize. You don't need to feel aroused to start. Trust that your interest will increase as you get going. But you will need, above all, to talk to your significant other. Not only about sex, what you do and don't like, but how close you are and how your relationship is doing. Is your man doing his share of the housework? There's considerable research showing that women over thirty feel more sexual interest in a partner who's handy with a vacuum cleaner. How convenient is that? Do you know how you're each doing at work? It's a myth that sex is a natural activity that anyone can do. After the first flush of youth, it's a game of skill. If you don't want a sexless relationship, you'll both have to work at regaining your interest.

Try Weakly

I am engaged to a man I met two years ago. We have the same understanding of how to live, but there is one big catch: the sexual chemistry is not fulfilling. My sex drive is higher than his, and the few times we do have sex rarely lead to orgasm for me. We have talked about this subject many times; his point is he just doesn't care about sex that much. He has mentioned that he thinks sex is dirty. Can I marry someone with whom I have this sort of issue?

The evidence is overwhelming that sexual difficulties cause conflict and unhappiness in relationships, and you sound pretty miserable already—so it probably would make sense to hold off on your wedding plans for the time being. It sounds like your romantic partner might be suffering from hypoactive sexual desire (HSD), one of many common sexual problems. According to a research paper published in the *British Medical Journal*, out of five hundred men visiting their doctors, one in five had a sexual problem. Difficulties with erections and loss of desire were the most common.

Sexual mythology would have us believe that men don't ever lose their desire for sex, but they do. There are many reasons for this lack of desire: illness (up to a third of the cases are caused by physical factors or side effects of medicines), stress, and sometimes a long-standing dislike of sex or lack of real physical attraction between couples. A survey of over eight hundred people by netdoctor.com found that a quarter had been brought up to think sex is "dirty" (not in a good way), so your fiancé is not unusual in his negativity. Sexual mythology would also have us believe that sexual chemistry makes sex effortless—it doesn't—so don't convince yourself that a lack of this ephemeral substance is to blame. However uncertain you are of the cause, make sure that it won't cause problems in your relationship. A study of seventy-two couples published in the *Archives of Sexual Behavior* found that those with the greatest differences in desire had the most unhappy relationships.

People with HSD don't tend to have sexual fantasies or feel much need to have sex. They may not understand how desire works and think it comes on like a light rather than developing as you're having sex. They may not associate feeling intimate with wanting sex, believing that only hard-core erotic feelings should initiate sex. People with HSD are often emotionally distanced, although this may be the effect rather than the cause of their problems. You sound rather detached from your fiancé too, and he may need as much love and understanding as you can bear to give him. Sex can bring you closer together, but you sometimes have to be intimate in the first place to want to have it.

So this is not about the quantity but the quality of sex and may not even be just about your fiancé. Sexual problems tend to involve two people, and in a third of couples where HSD is an issue the other partner will have their sexual difficulties too. The fact that you are compatible in other ways is encouraging and may make you both motivated enough to sort out your sexual problems.

You've got a lot to work out, and you will need help. Pre-marital counseling (or an approachable family doctor) is a good start, as sex may only be part of the problem. It's certainly a better place to start working on your relationship than at your wedding reception.

Dream On

My partner enjoys telling me about his sexual fantasies. They often involve someone who isn't me, which irritates me. Is this something men do more than women?

Most people have sexual fantasies, but they shouldn't feel compelled to share them. Fantasies are private thoughts and can be sexually inhibiting as well as liberating. Taking offense at a fantasy, however, invests it with too much meaning. It's just a thought (unless it really is depraved, in which case phone the police). If the fantasy is about a friend of yours, it's best if your partner keeps it to himself, as this type of fantasy goes down particularly badly. But it is still just a fantasy.

There are hundreds of books on sexual fantasies, so the subject certainly generates interest. And it isn't a male preserve; the sexologist Nancy Friday has made a living from her bestselling books on female fantasies, titled *My Secret Garden* and *Forbidden Flowers* (get the theme?).

Studies show what you'd expect, though: there are differences between the sexes, with men having more fantasies. A study by researchers at the University of Vermont of nearly 350 people whose ages ranged from eighteen to seventy (all either students or faculty at another university in New England, so this wasn't a study representative of most people) found

143

that nearly all of the men in their sample and 80 percent of the women had sexual fantasies about people who weren't their significant other. So not only men but also most women fantasize about sex, which is interesting as nearly half of the respondents in a *New York Times* poll in 2000 said that it was "not okay" to fantasize about having sex with someone else.

Women were more likely than men in the Vermont study to fantasize about a former partner—although these fantasies were uncommon. The longer people had been in a relationship, and the more partners they'd had, the more likely they were to fantasize about someone else. The average length of time people in the study had been in relationships was nine years and four months. So you may not like your partner's fantasizing, but it's normal and you shouldn't feel jealous. The study did find that people who fantasized about other people were more likely to have been unfaithful to their partner. But that doesn't prove one causes the other—so don't get upset. Unfaithfulness in this study was also broadly defined; it included kissing, which may not be everyone's idea of full-blown infidelity.

Men and women may not be aroused by each other's fantasies because their fantasies may be different. This is shown in other studies that suggest that men's fantasies focus more on the act of having sex, with less emotion and romance, than women's do. A study by researchers at the University of California at Berkeley and published in the *Journal of Sex Research* asked 162 people between the ages of twenty-one and forty-five to write sexual fantasies (as part of their research into links between power in sexual fantasies and the acceptance of myths about rape) and found that men's fantasies were more explicit, involved more sexual partners, and had themes of dominance. But men were also likely to fantasize about their partners being easily pleased and aroused. So your partner is also likely to have fantasies in which you're having a sexually amazing time. You may need to remind him that in real life more effort is needed to achieve these fantasies—and they're really the only ones you want to hear about.

Addicted to Love

My friend's boyfriend is continually unfaithful to her—one of us even caught him having sex with someone else at a party. However, he's now told her he's a sex addict. He says he loves her and will join a sex addicts' support group. Isn't "sex addiction" a pathetic excuse for his inability to be faithful? Shouldn't my friend just leave him?

It will be hard for your friend to stay with her boyfriend if he keeps having sex with other people. Most people really don't like that. Whether or not the cause is his "addiction" to sex is more debatable. The field of sex addiction is a hotbed of academic argument: some people say that it is like drug addiction; others maintain that it is compulsive behavior (akin to obsessively washing your hands for hours); and still others argue that it's a form of behavior that's impulsive or out of control. What no one disputes is that this preoccupation with sex damages relationships. People who claim to be addicted to sex will say that their everyday life is devoted to having sex. They can't stop looking for ever more partners (including paying for sex) or more pornography or both. Sexual addiction makes people sexualize ordinary events, use others for sex in a selfish way, and increasingly feel disgusted with themselves. Instead of going to work, seeing their partner, meeting up with friends, or doing their tax return, they will be looking for or having sex, with themselves if no one else is around.

However, sexuality is such a variable thing that the condition is also likely to overlap with the behavior of relatively normal (albeit sometimes sexually selfish) people. Some people are highly sexual and like to have orgasms several times a day. However, self-confessed sex addicts don't like what they're doing and may feel compelled to have sex when they feel depressed or anxious. Sex is not about pleasure for them but about filling an emotional void. Forgive this short simplistic description; there are textbooks for those who are really interested, but, unlike abnormal sexual stuff, like feeling up strangers, there's no agreed psychiatric definition.

A paper in the journal *Postgraduate Medicine* puts the rate of sex addiction at 3 to 6 percent. There is more research from the United States that points to the same rates. Surveys show that some people having out-of-control sex were abused as children—between one-third and two-thirds (although this abuse is not defined). Up to two-thirds of people having out-of-control sex have other addictions.

Treatments vary and are contentious, such as a twelve-step program adapted from the successful one used by Alcoholics Anonymous but with abstinence for only thirty to ninety days (the program includes a masturbation ban that online discussion forums suggest is usually broken). Total abstinence from sex would be somewhat limiting in life. A combination of drugs, sometimes to treat depression and anxiety, and talking therapies can help, but there isn't a cure and people do remain at risk of repeating their behaviors. It's up to your friend to decide whether she can stay with him—some couples do manage—but she will need to have huge reserves of understanding, forgiveness, and supportive friends.

Sex Toys

> My wife and I are around fifty years old and love each other very much, but our sex life—particularly when our children were younger—has always had its highs and lows. Two years ago in an attempt to rekindle our sex life I bought her a vibrator, which I had hoped we could use together. However, I'm now worried that the idea may have backfired on me, as I know she uses it but seems to want to make love with me even less frequently.

How nice of you to get her a vibrator. Unfortunately, she's found out (presuming she hadn't used one before) that it's much easier to have an orgasm with a vibrator than with another human being. In fact, for many women, whatever they use, it's easier to have an orgasm on their own.

Contrary to popular belief, people over fifty want to and do have sex. A study of sexuality in five hundred older women by researchers at the Royal Brisbane and Women's Hospital in Australia found that over half of them between the ages of forty and eighty were having sex, often a few times a month. But the news wasn't all good, especially for Australian men. The researchers found that 56 percent of women who were sexually active without a partner had an orgasm every time they masturbated, compared with only 24 percent of women having sex with a partner. This may seem obvious—the former is not an activity people usually start without finishing—but it suggests that some men are not as careful or skillful in stimulating their partners as they might be. No one is saying that ordinary mortals can provide the intense stimulation of a vibrator—although a study by researchers at the City University of New York into the quality and speed of orgasm using different types of vibrators still found variations, such as reaching orgasm in twenty seconds versus an hour. But a partner should offer a more well-rounded, intimate sexual experience (a vibrator can't be romantic), and this is what you would hope your wife wants. What you need to ask (yourself, but her in particular) is whether you have satisfying sex with each other.

As women and men get older, their desire for sex can trail off a bit. They may feel less attractive or have health problems that make sex more of an effort. After menopause, sex is just harder for women sometimes; it takes longer for blood to get to the right parts and for lubrication to kick in. Sex toys eliminate the need to feel desire, as all you have to do is turn them on, but there's a risk in that the instant gratification is more mechanical than emotional.

All couples have sex lives that ebb and flow, but you need to ask how emotionally close you are now (after all these years) and how affectionate you are to each other. The same issues that affect the sex lives of younger couples apply to older ones as well. If your sex life has become boring or unfulfilling, or if you are no longer emotionally close, you need to find out or you'll never dislodge that vibrator. If you're intimate enough to buy her a vibrator in the first place, you should be able to do that.

Just for the Celibate

My husband and I have stopped having sex. I'm not sure why we have embraced celibacy, but our marriage has been sexless for about a year (I know he's not having an affair). We've both been struggling at work and with our teenage children, so I'm not sure I miss it. He doesn't seem bothered, but how can our relationship last if we never have sex together again?

If you don't know why you've become a celibate couple, you can try the usual reasons. Dr. Denise Donnelly's study of 6,029 married people in the *Journal of Sex Research* found that couples were less likely to have sex if they were unhappy (hard to know which came first, it's reciprocal), had small children, and didn't do much together. Infidelity, illness, concerns about appearance, and getting older can also put people off sex, as can pregnancy. All things considered, it's amazing that couples ever have sex. But they do, and when celibacy usurps sex it is rarely by mutual decision or a matter that is fully discussed. When it does happen, it usually leaves one person feeling rejected, frustrated, and unhappy.

You need to figure out if you're what one self-help Web site calls an "incel." This is short for "involuntary celibate" (incelsite.com). You would qualify if you wanted sex, in this case with your husband, but couldn't have it, either because "the spark" (that elusive core of modern marriages) had gone out, or he didn't want it anymore. Or could *he* be the incel and you're the one who's okay with no sex? Unfortunately, as you suspect, your relationship may not be in sound shape. Another study by Donnelly of seventy-seven incels in marriages or long-term relationships published in the *Journal of Marriage and Family* used a Web-based questionnaire to ask people why they stayed in their sexless relationships (defined in this case as no sex for six months). This study was not representative of the general population, because not everyone uses the Internet (really, they don't), and these people came from an online discussion group. But it's not easy to find incels, so the results are still useful. Over 64 percent of people said that sex had gradually tailed off for them (from a mixture of tiredness and lack of interest). As a result, around 26 percent had had affairs, one-third had had therapy (but generally didn't feel it helped), and only a third were reconciled to a celibate relationship. Incels spoke of being unhappy and feeling incomplete without sex.

Your relationship may last without sex, but you couldn't bet on it being better. The longer you go without sex, the less you miss it; so don't kid yourself that it's a considered choice. Donnelly's study found that half the people said their ideal partner was their current one—if only they'd have sex again. Other studies show that most often it's the man who decides to stop having sex, usually without discussing it first and sometimes because it's more difficult for him to have an erection or feel sexually interested. If that's true for you, at least talk to your husband about it and try to rekindle your sex life. It may feel like an enormous effort to start with, but it's so, so much easier in the long run.

It's Width Not Length

I've been worried about my penis being smaller than other guys' since I was at school, but my girlfriend says I'm nuts and it is fine. Statistics suggest it is average in size, and I've heard thickness rather than length matters most to women. Is that true, and can you make a penis bigger?

Lots of men worry about the size of their penis. But the odds are that you are within the normal range given by one study or another. A study by researchers for Lifestyles Condom Company of three hundred men found that two-thirds of penises were between 5.1 and 6.2 inches long when erect. The penises were measured by nurses rather than by the men themselves, so this study is more likely to be accurate than those that rely on men doing it themselves. The erect penis is not easy to measure, but you can try to do it by using a tape measure from the base of the penis where it touches the pubic bone (press in especially if you have a paunch there) to the tip. Some experts suggest that measuring a penis by stretching it when flaccid is an even more accurate guide to how long it will be when erect. The famous Kinsey Institute's *New Report on Sex* says that the average man's erect penis is five to seven inches long and has a circumference of four to six inches. The rule of thumb is that an erect penis is twice the size of a flaccid one.

Men seem to underestimate the size of their own penis and overestimate the size of everyone else's. This is because you look down on your penis, literally, but sideways at other men's. Look at yours sideways in the mirror, and your worry may evaporate; it's instantly bigger. A study published in the *International Journal of Impotence Research* in Italy of sixty-seven men asking for surgical enhancement found that none of them had abnormally small penises. Once shown where their penises stood on a graph (in the normal range), forty-eight men (72 percent) went away happily but nineteen (28 percent) still wanted surgery. The researchers offered psychosexual counseling first, but only eleven agreed (the surgeons would not do surgery without counseling first) and the study doesn't say how many men eventually had the operation (although considerably fewer than the sixty-seven who initially asked for it). Studies show that even men with true micropenises (which affects less than one in two hundred men) have good sex lives. Surgery is unlikely to help any man whose penis is a normal size anyway.

The sex-research pioneers William Masters and Virginia E. Johnson said size didn't matter because the vagina accommodates what is offered. A study published in the *British Medical Journal* of magnetic resonance imaging of couples having sex shows the base of the penis taking up a lot of the room (thereby helping clitoral stimulation) and the penis bending into a boomerang shape. Length may look more enticing (too long, and it can look threatening), but the reality is that most of it isn't needed. Girth, however, does seem to be important. A small study of fifty women between the ages of eighteen and twenty-five by researchers at the University of Texas-Pan American found that forty-five said width was more important than length.

If you still want to know if there is anything that makes penises longer, the answer is no, not really. You can cut ligaments so the penis dangles more (but isn't really longer), inject fat into the penis (which can make it lumpy), and wear frames that extend the penis. Suction pumps make penises swollen but sore. There are other surgical techniques, but results are mediocre and the procedures carry some risk.

As for women, they don't really care. Better to invest in some thoughtful foreplay techniques than fret about penile enhancement. A penis is not nearly as important as the thoughtful and skillful lover attached to it.

Save Sex

I am seventeen years old, and most of my friends have had sex. I don't feel ready to lose my virginity. My mom says that when she was young, people waited longer before having sex. Isn't it better for a relationship if you wait?

Sexual attitudes have changed since your mom's time. Most people do have sex for the first time at about age seventeen according to the Guttmacher Institute, but that doesn't mean you have to. By the age of fifteen only 13 percent of teens will have had sex, though the number rises to seven in ten by the time they reach nineteen years of age. The Economic and Social Research Council (ESRC) says that the median age at which people have sex for the first time has fallen roughly four years in the past forty years. So people did wait longer in the past, especially before the pill came along.

The downside of having sex early is the risk of sexually transmitted diseases. About one in four young adults ages fifteen to twenty-four catches a sexually transmitted disease every year. The Centers for Disease Control and Prevention estimates that 35 percent of thirteen- to nineteen-year-olds are infected with human papillomavirus (HPV). If these statistics are not enough to kill your passion, cast your mind over the prospect of teen pregnancy. For every thousand girls who are having sex, eighty-four will become pregnant. So arguably we're not very good at having sex young—one reason for waiting.

Also, sex, like most other things, gets better with practice, so it's unlikely to be a great success from the start. The research shows that however cool it is to view sex as a recreational activity, it is usually best with someone you know, like, trust, can talk to, and be uncool with. You may not need to wait long to find someone like that, but you'll have a better time if you do.

Call me old-fashioned, but I don't see why there's a rush. If peer-group pressure becomes unbearable, you can always be vague—it's not uncommon for people to exaggerate their sexual experience. Once you're dating there shouldn't be a rush however young or old you are. A MORI poll for London's

Observer showed that out of 1,618 people, 18 percent of women waited over two months before having sex in a relationship (but only half the sample answered; most said that the time varied). In your mom's youth a study from East Carolina University in Greenville, North Carolina, of 555 students found that three-quarters of the women felt petting should wait until the fourth date, while almost one-third of the men thought it should occur on the first date. Things generally went slower back then.

The ESRC report says that women are twice as likely as men to regret the first time they had sex and three times as likely as men to say they were less willing than their partners. So it's perfectly sensible not to have sex before you are ready. Sex is so ubiquitous that it may seem strange to a potential boyfriend that there's anything you need to wait for. But that doesn't mean you can't wait if you want to.

Neurotic Erotic

I caught my boyfriend of nine months looking at porn on the Internet the other night. I asked him how often he did this and he said not much, but I'm not sure if I believe him. I was really upset, but now I think maybe I'm overreacting and that lots of men do this. Do they?

Lots of men do look at porn online, but that doesn't mean you can't get upset if your boyfriend is one of them. You should know, however, that it is a common male pastime. A survey by Nielsen/NetRatings shows that one in four men between the ages of twenty-five and forty-nine has visited an adult porn site in the past month. Other surveys put the percentage at more like 60 percent. Ask men, and they will say they're surprised these figures are so low. Who wouldn't take a peek if it's freely available?

Porn on the Internet can vary from the type found in men's magazines to the more nasty stuff—I'm assuming your boyfriend was looking at mainstream porn, and some women are fairly relaxed about their men doing this. A study of one hundred women whose partners used pornography, published in the *Journal of Sex and Marital Therapy*, found that most weren't bothered but that one-quarter to one-third were distressed by it. These women felt their partners had been unfaithful to them by looking at pornography, especially when the women they were lusting over had 40DD breasts. They worried that in comparison they were overweight and unsexy (and who wouldn't be?) and hence not good enough. Some took their insecurity one step further and asked themselves if their partners used pornography because they themselves were so undesirable. (The research shows this isn't true; most men who look at porn do so because it's available.) They also worried that their partners used pornography because they found their sex lives unfulfilling. Women with feminist tendencies, who felt that porn objectifies women, wondered if this was how their partners really felt about them.

But Dr. Ana Bridges, who carried out the study, thinks that most men who use porn do so just because it's there. It most likely says nothing about how they feel about their partners or their relationships; they just like the visual stimulation. Bridges estimates that in a quarter of relationships porn use may mean something, but it's hard to say what.

Bearing in mind that the use of pornography may or may not mean something, you can try to work out why you're upset and take a practical rather than moral approach. People vary in all sorts of ways, including in what they find arousing. Is your relationship otherwise happy? Are you having enough sex (as men who use porn can get lazy and just have sex with themselves), and is it good sex? You need to talk to your partner and let him know you're upset. He may be able to convince you that it's fine for him to use porn whenever he likes, or the two of you could negotiate to set some limits. For example, maybe you think it's okay if he watches porn when you're out but not when you're in the next room (and hence available). Be clear about what you agree to, but don't monitor his use because it will end in tears.

The Nielsen/NetRatings survey showed that women also liked visual stimulation, with 1.4 million a year looking at on-line porn. Men may be as unhappy as women about their partners engaging in this activity. Other surveys show that just as many men as women feel insecure when their partner looks at porn. Bridges suggests that couples take pictures of each other for visual stimulation, but only if they trust each other to never post them on the Internet.

Born to Use Porn?

> I enjoy pornography. I'd really like my girlfriend to watch it with me, because I think it would make our sex more exciting. She doesn't seem that interested. I've watched pornography with other girlfriends. How can I get her to try it?

It's an individual thing, liking or not liking pornography. Most pornography is made for and marketed to men, and studies show that men start using porn earlier than women and are more enthusiastic about it. Some feminists have argued either that porn exploits women or that it arouses them but they're too repressed to admit it. What's certain is that discussions about porn are usually loaded with morality.

Figures for the use of pornography by women are not terribly robust. Dr. Clarissa Smith, author of the book *One for the Girls!* and senior lecturer in media and cultural studies at the University of Sunderland in England, says that 40 percent is an accepted estimate. This figure is based on a Nielsen / NetRatings survey of women's use of pornography on the Web in 2006. However, a review article in *Archives of Sexual Behavior* says that out of the 40 million adults accessing pornography Web sites annually, 72 percent are men and 28 percent women. Smith's own research, interviewing women who bought *For Women* (a porn magazine for women), found that they mostly looked at the magazine on their own; they didn't want to be distracted while they were being aroused. Smith says that women shouldn't be coerced into watching porn just because their partner wants to, but if you can interest your girlfriend, try porn films for couples by such female directors as Candida Royalle and Anna Span. Span's view is that women want better-looking men and more soap opera in their porn. They also like their porn stars to have better clothes and accessories.

The most rigorous research in this area has been carried out in Denmark, a country unencumbered by guilt about pornography. Gert Martin Hald's study of 688 men and women (ages eighteen to thirty) published in the *Archives of Sexual Behavior* found that almost all men and 80 percent of women had used porn at least once—50 percent of the women in the past month. Hald's definition of pornography was that it had to include "explicit exposure or description of the genitals," but it also had to show actual intercourse; browsing through *Playboy* or *Playgirl* didn't count. Women were more likely to watch pornography with a partner than on their own—twice as likely as men were. Hald's view is that it isn't shame that stops women from being as turned on by porn as men; they just think about sex differently. Most porn, he says, is used by men to masturbate and shows an easily available woman that they don't have to invest in at all. Thin plots about pizza delivery men turning up and getting sex on demand usually do more for men than women.

Once you've asked your girlfriend to watch porn with you, you shouldn't keep asking if she says no. It won't be helpful for your sex life to make her feel guilty and repressed. If she isn't interested, you'll have to think of other ways to boost your sex lives. Traditionally, sex with feelings is a winner for women. And you could still dress up as the pizza delivery man.

8

Surviving Children

Bundle of Joy?

> My partner is convinced that having a baby will ruin both our relationship and his life. Is there any evidence to show he could be right? Can the arrival of a baby split apart an otherwise blissfully happy couple?

Couples often think that a baby will make them even more blissful. But they'd be wrong. For most couples, babies can be bad news. There's a lot of research on the "transition to parenthood," and some of it is contradictory. But a meta-analytic study of the quality of relationships after children, published in the *Journal of Marriage and Family*, added up results from ninety studies (covering 31,331 people) to find out. The authors discovered that couples with children were generally less happy than nonparents. Women with children under one were the least happy, only 38 percent of them having higher than average levels of satisfaction with their relationships compared to 62 percent who hadn't yet had children. Men didn't show reduced levels of bliss until the second year of the baby's life, although by the time the child was two both men and women were feeling better about their relationships.

The reasons are obvious. Babies deprive you of sleep—which in itself causes conflict. They erode your time together and mess up your sex life, and women still usually bear the brunt of child-care responsibilities and are more likely to feel ground down and resentful (especially if they are combining motherhood with a career). The study also found that the more children a couple had, the less happy they were likely to be. Other studies show that conflict doesn't end when children get past the toddling stage; it's the teenage years that can be the most challenging.

So what's the good news? Well, children do bring joy, and the research, while not conclusive, suggests that on a personal level they make the people who have them more rather than less happy. And if you are a blissful couple to start with, it definitely helps. A study of eighty-two couples, published in the *Journal of Family Psychology*, found that those with good relationships were protected from the challenges of having babies. Couples who weren't critical of each other but gently tried to solve problems together, couples who were affectionate, and, in particular, couples where the father helped out were the happiest after having a baby. These results support findings from other studies that show parents who compete for their child's attention and undermine each other's parenting are more likely to be unhappy. A big predictor of happiness is whether the decision to have a baby was mutual. So be warned—especially as children don't thrive when their parents are constantly fighting.

I hope your relationship can withstand a baby. But forewarned is forearmed. The organization One Plus One has an excellent pamphlet called *The Transition to Parenthood—The Magic Moment*, which says that babies tend neither to cause good-quality relationships to deteriorate nor to bring unhappy couples any closer together. The pamphlet quotes some researchers who found an increase in relationship satisfaction ranging from 18 to 30 percent when couples become parents. Most important, the research shows that couples do better if they know what's coming.

Changing Minds

> I would love to have children, but my partner has said that he doesn't want them. I almost wish we'd never discussed the subject and that I had just got pregnant. If I did get pregnant, wouldn't he come around to the idea?

The trouble is that your partner would have to come around to the baby itself, not just the idea. On the one hand, you can curse yourself for bringing the subject up. According to a study in the medical journal the *Lancet*, at least one-third of pregnancies in the United Kingdom are unplanned, so you could have presented him with a scenario that goes, "Oh no, the condom must have split," or "I should never have taken those antibiotics with my pill." But on the other hand, it's worth knowing how your significant other feels about having children because children disrupt relationships. We know this because the research keeps telling us so. According to a large review of ninety-seven studies with 47,692 people in the *Journal of Marriage and Family*, people who are "married with kids" have less satisfying relationships than those who are married without them. However, children are a deterrent to breaking up, at least initially, so this influence may skew the results. Even so, overall 55 percent of couples without children had higher than average levels of happiness with their relationship compared with 45 percent of parents. The extra work, sleep deprivation, and loss of freedom all take their toll, however cute the baby is.

So you really *did* have to ask your partner how he felt about being a father. Studies show that men can be underwhelmed by having children, expecting to enjoy fatherhood much more than they do. Men often feel more anxious about providing for their children financially; so instead of bonding with their baby, they may work inappropriately late at the office.

The research clearly shows that men who do not want a pregnancy—let alone a baby at the end of it—are unlikely to be enthusiastic about it. A study of 6,816 fathers who lived with their babies measured how often they changed diapers and comforted the baby when it cried (nurturing activities), how much they held and tickled the baby (warmth activities), and whether the pregnancy was wanted or not. About 8 percent of the fathers did not want the pregnancy, and 20 percent wanted it but not just yet, thanks. The study found that having a baby didn't bring fathers around; those that hadn't wanted the baby were much less likely to hold their baby or be affectionate toward it.

Fathers are more likely to get involved as children grow up, and some research suggests that they're more involved if they have a son. They are also more involved if their relationship with their mate is strong and happy. A relationship is unlikely to be happy if it is built on unilateral decision making. You need to talk about what having a baby really means—the impact it will have on your lifestyle, ambitions, and relationship. Such a chat is fair to your mate, and it's fair to the baby you want to have, who would (I'm guessing) prefer to be wanted by both its parents.

Impact of Infertility

> We're finally giving up trying for a baby after many years and trying to accept a child-free life. Our infertility was "unexplained," and we've been through traumatic times but still stayed together. But what will happen to us now that we've given up the hope of having children? Will our relationship and lives recover from this loss?

Infertility is immensely distressing. The tests and treatment are stressful, and it can take years to grieve for the children you expected to have. What the research does seem to show, however, is that couples do survive.

Between 10 and 17 percent of couples have some infertility problems, according to a paper published in the journal *Human Reproduction* from researchers at Helsinki University Central Hospital. Regardless of who has the problem, the research shows that couples do better when they feel the same way about their infertility (equally sad, angry, or accepting). You also do better if you tell each other how you feel, but of course you knew that.

The problem is the time it takes to readjust your lives. In a study published in the *Journal of Counselling and Development*, thirty-seven couples from Canadian cities who had stopped fertility treatments were asked how they were coping at ten-month intervals. It took up to three years, of exhaustion and hopelessness (mostly during the first ten months), frustration and anger (some felt they had put their lives on hold to have children), before they could feel optimistic about life again. Although couples questioned their relationships, many said they'd grown closer. The study was small, however, and didn't say how many couples stayed together.

Being sensitive to each other's feelings is easier said than done if you're crying your eyes out. A study published in the journal *Family Relations* of 420 couples who were still having fertility treatments found that women were most distressed when their husbands distanced themselves and men found it hard to cope when their wives kept their feelings to themselves. Couples who were best able to support each other were those who didn't blame themselves or each other for the fertility problems. How you cope will also depend partly on your family's expectations for you and on your feelings about adoption and surrogacy. Infertility organizations suggest joining support groups and couples counseling.

I couldn't find any evidence that infertility increases the risk of divorce. But more important, neither could Professor Arthur L. Greil, a sociologist and expert in this area from Alfred University in New York. Couples, he tells me, get stressed, but many say their relationships grow stronger. The relationships are likely to be as happy (and that includes being as sexually fulfilling) as anyone else's—however hard this may be for you to believe right now.

Seasonal Birth Disorders

We are trying for a baby. We know we may not be able to engineer exactly when I get pregnant, but if we could pick a time of year, what's the best month to have a baby?

The answer is that it depends who's asking. The answer for the baby may be different from the one for the woman who's carrying it. Panting in the summer heat with a swollen belly that hides even bigger ankles is uncomfortable for a woman. But on the other hand, a study from researchers at the University of Southampton in England that looked at 1,750 men and women born in Hertfordshire over one decade found men born in winter had an increased risk of obesity. You wouldn't want to wish that on your baby, now, would you? Figures from the UK Office for National Statistics show that babies born in winter may also have an increased risk of being stillborn and dying before they're a month old. However, these tragic events are rare, and no one would suggest you avoid a winter birth because of them.

Most research into the "seasonality" effects of birth doesn't look at whether it's more pleasant to push a stroller through autumnal leaves or spring showers. It looks for more heavyweight things, such as links between birthdays and serious illnesses. Researchers have looked for and found some seasonal links with Parkinson's disease (spring), multiple sclerosis (10 percent more in May, according to a study in the *British Medical Journal*), epilepsy (winter), brain tumors (January/February), celiac disease (summer), and risk of suicide (April, May, and June). There are many other studies on other diseases, but the strength of most of these associations is not clear, and it seems that most months have some theoretical risk attached to them.

Other factors are a greater worry. For example, children born late in the school year tend to struggle to keep up with their peers academically. A study from the Institute of Fiscal Studies in the UK confirms this, finding that children born in August do worse in school tests for most of their academic careers and are more likely to drop out at the age of sixteen. This isn't the fault of August but of these babies' relative young age in relation to their classmates. At the age of eleven, August-born girls are two-thirds more likely than other children to have a diagnosed learning difficulty. As the general secretary of the Association of School and College Leaders in England was quoted as saying, "You don't do your children any favors by having them in July or August." But on the other hand, the weather is better and you can go for walks.

Well, parents don't seem to be doing their children any favors—federal statistics show that August is the top month for having babies. September and July are close behind. This ties in nicely with the winter-nights hypothesis, where couples can't watch television night after night and so become bored enough—and because it's winter, cold enough—to resort to sex. (Everyone knows that hot weather doesn't make you sexually insatiable, it just makes you sweaty and grumpy.) This pattern of winter sex giving rise to summer births is seen in some European countries. In the Netherlands the organization that collects these figures, Statistics Netherlands, reports that the most common months for babies' births are July, August, and September.

If you do plan when to give birth, you must possess advanced organizational skills. This quality alone bodes well for you, whatever month you have your baby in.

Kids as Contraceptives

My husband and I have a two-and-a-half-year-old and a six-month-old baby (whom I still breast-feed). My husband is unhappy with the amount of sex we have. He says the average is three times a week, but we should be doing it five times to make up for lost time (pregnancy, postbirth). I say leave me alone so I can sleep while there's a chance. I don't want to ask the other mothers at playgroup, but what's everyone else doing?

Most mothers of young children aren't looking for more sex. They're desperate for sleep, not for the chance to catch up on the erotic action they missed out on while heavily pregnant and during the months immediately after giving birth. You need to know that the average your husband is quoting is not for parents. It's for childless couples in their early twenties.

The amount of sex that people have varies according to many factors, such as whether they're single (less sex), whether they've been with someone a long time (longer usually means less), how old they are (less over the age of fifty), whether they're worried about something (who isn't?—and it's less), and whether they have children (less again, when the children are young). Most married couples have sex around seven times a month according to the National Health and Social Life Survey. Couples under twenty-five have sex eleven times a month (apparently still not enough for your husband).

Having children, especially young ones, undoubtedly reduces a couple's sexual activity. A recent survey of twenty thousand parents conducted by the Web site BabyCenter found that six months after the birth of the baby the average frequency of sex was three to five times a month. A study of 570 women and 550 of their partners in the *Journal of Sexual Research* found that couples had sex four to five times a month during pregnancy, stopped for seven weeks after the birth, and then went back to midpregnancy levels of sex by the time their babies were four months old. It took a year for them to feel the sex was as good as it had been before the baby arrived.

Other studies have found that even after a year, up to 95 percent of couples still have less sex than before the pregnancy. Breast-feeding, however, does not seem to reduce the amount of sex that couples have.

Survey data aren't that much help, because couples set their own levels of sexual activity and that's what they expect. They do, however, support the notion that men often want more sex than they're getting. (Does quality count for nothing?) A survey of over eight hundred adults by the health Web site Netdoctor found that nearly 80 percent of men thought they weren't getting enough sex (compared with 60 percent of women).

Babies and energetic children (are there any other kind?) reduce passion because they cause exhaustion. Your husband is clearly getting too much sleep if he's feeling passionate most nights of the week. Sex drives vary, and you don't say if your husband has always wanted more sex than you have wanted. But you need to negotiate with him not only on how much sex the two of you have but also on how much sleep he can help you to get (by helping out with the kids!).

Step to Take

My seventeen-year-old stepson takes my clothes and DVDs, comes in at 3:00 a.m., and sleeps until noon. He isn't in college, doesn't work, and is rude and selfish. My girlfriend doesn't seem to do anything about his behavior, although she knows I'm upset. We have a young daughter together, and this isn't good for her. How can I get my girlfriend to see that her son is ruining our relationship?

It's hard being the stepfather to a teenage son. You may, how-ever, have forgotten what you were like as a teenager; selfish-ness is part of the job description. The bad behavior should pass. Teenagers can be tough for anyone to like, but research shows that stepparents find it harder to do so than biological parents. Stepparents have a difficult, undefined role; they of-ten feel their parenting is undermined by the biological par-ent. Having their own children can make stepparents more intolerant of their stepchildren, as frequently they feel more fatherly or motherly toward their own children. It's a com-mon problem. According to the U.S. Census Bureau, 30 per-cent of American children live with a stepparent. In many countries the stepfamily will soon be the most common type of family (and in the United States, it already is).

Studies show that couples in stepfamilies struggle more than traditional families. A study by the Joseph Rowntree Foundation of 878 people bringing up children in stepfamilies found that both biological and stepparents had more relation-ship problems and argued more about how to bring up their children. Remarriages with stepchildren are more likely to break up than those without. But enough about the grown-ups—it's harder for the stepchildren too. The Children's Soci-ety, a charity in the United Kingdom, says that stepchildren are twice as likely as other kids to run away from home. It may be uncomfortable to acknowledge, but there's considerable re-search showing that stepparents are less warm and supporting of stepchildren; put simply, less interested in them. This gets worse when they have their own children with their partner—largely because younger children need close monitoring. However, other studies are more optimistic, showing that relationships can grow closer over time, although adolescence is usually a low point.

Your girlfriend knows that you're upset and that her son's behavior is unacceptable, but she has a loyalty to her son that you don't share. She may suspect you'd be more accommodating if your own daughter was behaving this way, whatever you say. She may also question whether you were sufficiently interested in him earlier to make it all right for you to be so angry now. You can't ignore that. But if the two of you argue over his behavior, this will make your stepson's behavior worse.

His behavior alone is not ruining your relationship; it's also how you're dealing with it. You and your girlfriend need to negotiate a united front and set boundaries for your stepson that you both enforce. It's not good for him to live nocturnally and have no structure to his life. He may be a selfish seventeen-year-old, but he may not be a very happy one. If his biological father has a good relationship with him, get Dad involved. Some families set up behavioral contracts with their teenagers that include rewards as well as sanctions, and you can get some help with organizations that work with families to develop these. Such contracts can help set boundaries and ensure that as a family you keep talking to each other. You should try to develop some relationship with your stepson, even as you hunt for your favorite T-shirt on his filthy floor. If it's any comfort, some middle-aged men might even be flattered that a teenager wants to wear their clothes.

For the Kids

I have been unhappy with my husband for years, and our marriage is effectively over. We don't fight much, though there's no affection or attraction between us; but he's a good dad, and the children would be devastated if we divorced. Is it better to wait until the children leave home before we break up?

Deciding to divorce is not a trivial decision, but neither is staying in an unhappy marriage for the sake of the children. A report from the National Marriage Project in the United States cites a national survey in 1993 that found only 15 percent of people agreed with the statement, "When there are children in the family, parents should stay together even if they don't get along." The bar for not getting along has been lowered over the years.

But if you are going to put your children's happiness above your own, you will want to know that staying together is measurably better for them. Particularly when so many couples don't seem to be doing it. The UK Office for National Statistics reports that 10 percent of all families are stepfamilies and almost one in four children lives in a single-parent family. In the United States, a paper in the journal *Social Work* in 2003 estimated that around one-third of the population are part of a stepfamily. There is a huge amount of research on the effects of divorce on children, and although some children do fantastically well afterward, the pointers are mostly in the opposite direction.

One study on delaying divorce, from the University of Pennsylvania and the London School of Economics, used data from 11,407 people who took part in the National Child Development Study. The people in the study were thirty-three years old and divided into two groups: those who were children (seven to sixteen) when their parents divorced and those who were older. The people whose parents had divorced when they were children performed worse in school and were more likely to be poor and have children early in life. But the researchers argue that all studies overstate the effects of divorce because they fail to take into account how the children were brought up in the family before the divorce.

There isn't strong evidence that delaying divorce prevents serious fallout, although the overall effects of divorce include, according to a report from the Vanier Institute of the Family, an increased risk of poverty, depression, doing poorly at school, becoming a young offender, teenage pregnancy, and relationship problems. The report does say, however, that when you compare these misfortunes in children of divorced parents versus those from intact families, the average differences are not huge. On a more mundane level, children miss the other parent. Sometimes terribly. The Vanier Institute report also says that although divorces that end parental conflict can have positive effects for children, in those families where parents have got along fairly well, a divorce can be shocking for the children because they never expected it.

Two parents are generally thought to be better than one if they support each other in bringing up their children. Divorce, it should be noted, is sufficiently stressful to make it hard to be a parent, at least for a while. If you are motivated enough to stay in this marriage for the children, is it so impossible to try to improve it for yourself? Talking to your husband, getting outside help (but you have to want to try), and seeing if you can salvage your marriage would be better for all of you.

9

Testing Times

First Feelings

Out of the blue I've had an e-mail from my first real girlfriend. We broke up when I went to college. She says she's happily married and just wanted to say hi, but I was quite shocked. I'm married with two children, and I'm not sure I should reply. Should I just press *DELETE*?

Yes, if you want to preserve the relationship you've already got. Early loves are incredibly powerful, and the Internet has made them increasingly accessible. A survey in *Time* magazine in 2000 found that out of over three thousand people nearly 60 percent said they often thought about their first loves. Dr. Nancy Kalish from California State University has done the bulk of research into what she calls "lost loves" following her own experience (it did not work out). In her 2004 survey of

1,300 randomly selected adults from all over the United States, one-third said they would reunite with their first loves if they could. She estimates that 10 percent of people try to get in touch with a lost love. There are no numbers for those who get in touch and within minutes remember exactly why they broke up in the first place.

By advertising in the media, Kalish has data on 2,500 couples who reunited. Most (around 84 percent) reunited with someone they'd loved before the age of twenty-two. Usually they'd split up because they'd been too young, moved away, or their parents had disapproved of the relationship. The reasons were external, usually out of their control, and had nothing to do with how well they got along, and many of the couples felt angry about the separation for years. People who broke up because they were cheated on, unhappy, or bored do not seem to go back for more.

The first one thousand couples Kalish found in the 1990s were mostly single when they located their lost loves. Once they met, things moved quickly, with 40 percent of them picking up where they had left off within three weeks. Most then married, with over 70 percent still together in 2004. (These figures may be skewed, because Kalish included everyone in her counting—even those married for a few months.) Couples said they felt emotionally intense and comfortable with each other. But the familiarity did not make things dull. Sexually, these couples felt more like they were slipping into red stilettos than beige slippers.

Why are these relationships so compelling? Psychiatrists at the University of California talk of early love experiences as being chemically hardwired into the brain. Your ex grew up with you, knows your family, and most likely set the standard for love. You shared friends, hopes, and cult television shows. There's a lot to talk about. These were not insignificant relationships at the time. Kalish found that many of the first loves she found had been together initially for two to five years and had mourned the relationship for anything up to three years.

But before you pull up that e-mail again, take note: Kalish's more recent couples, who are rather different from the earlier group that she researched, are not happy. Most have casually Googled in a speculative fashion, with no plan for what to do if they found their lost love. They were mostly already in committed, usually happy, relationships, and 80 percent ended up having affairs with their lost loves. Kalish hasn't finished analyzing the data but believes only a small proportion look likely to make the connection long-term. The destruction it causes families makes her almost evangelical in telling people not to press REPLY. Unless you are single. And you aren't.

Fatal Attraction

I was attracted to my boyfriend because he was gorgeous and easygoing. I have a high-powered job and I had liked his lack of ambition—but now it's driving me mad, and I'm embarrassed when he tells my friends he works in a thrift store and watches daytime television. Is it perverse for me to want to break up with him because of this? It's why I used to like him.

Gorgeous is always attractive and may explain any oversight in other areas. I don't know how long you've been a couple, but early in a relationship, both lust and being on your best behavior can get in the way of assessing long-term potential.

Falling for qualities you later detest is termed "fatal attraction" by the sociologist Diane Felmlee, who researched this phenomenon at the University of California at Davis. She lifted the term from the film *Fatal Attraction*, in which (for those who haven't seen it) an initially sexy and wild woman becomes a crazy bunny boiler. In research published in *Personal Relationships*, Felmlee asked 301 men and women (students attending college on the West Coast) to recall the last serious relationship they'd had that had broken up. She asked, what specific qualities did your ex have that attracted you initially? Further down in the questionnaire she asked, which ones did you find least attractive? A third of the participants cited looks, one in five a sense of humor, and 12 percent said intelligence. Only 2 percent of people were attracted to those who were easygoing, so you're in the minority there. But many qualities in retrospect had a downside (although you may want to take the results with a pinch of sour grapes because these were exes). The qualities most likely to be adored and later loathed were "exciting," "different," and—guess what?—"easygoing." "Confidence" became "arrogance," "funny" turned into "immature," and "spontaneous" became "weird." Even characteristics that you'd think everyone would love, like "caring," became twisted into "possessive." The more people raved about a quality, the more likely it was later to end up on the things-I-hate-most list. When someone called a quality unique, this characteristic was three times more likely than others to be one of the reasons for ending the relationship.

One-third of participants reported breaking up with someone because of a quality that they no longer found attractive. In particular, the differences between couples ("he's so easygoing, and I am so ambitious") that are initially attractive become more noticeable and annoying once that first attraction is over. Also, studies show that the length of a relationship is related to the support the couple gets from friends and family. If your friends are all very high-powered and career-oriented, they may subtly or blatantly undermine your relationship. They may never be able to see what you saw in him.

Only you know if you want someone who is more ambitious. At least start talking to him about how you feel. Not in a critical way, but as a genuine attempt to see if this disenchantment is real. Relationships do fluctuate, especially in the early days. You may be surprised. He may think you want him to be home when you arrive after a long workday, and you may find he really craves a job in high finance. Felmlee's study found one woman who complained her ex had been too sweet and sensitive. She found out how wrong she was when he went out with her best friend shortly after they broke up.

Fingers to the Bone

My partner doesn't appreciate how much housework and running around after the kids I do. We both work full-time, and my job is as busy as his. How can I get him to stop taking what I do at home for granted?

There's an old-fashioned saying that goes, "I like hugs, I like kisses, but what I love is help with the dishes"—and sadly it still has a certain resonance. A Pew Research Center survey in 2007 of two thousand Americans found that sharing household chores was given as the third most popular factor for a happy marriage. It came ahead of money, a nice house, and even having children. A total of 62 percent said it was important, compared to only 7 percent who thought it didn't matter. Sharing household chores is now nipping at the heels of the second most highly rated factor: a good sex life. Faithfulness was number one. And if you're a woman, the amount of sex you have and the amount of housework your significant other does may not be unrelated. Some women find "chore-play," as it's called when men do housework, makes them more sexually interested in their partner. Not because dusting is erotic but because sharing household tasks makes for fairer relationships and intimacy, which is erotic. No wonder that a coffee-table book called *Porn for Women*, which has hunky men, fully dressed, in aprons, doing housework, has sold so well.

The amount of housework that men do has been rising steadily. According to the Council on Contemporary Families in the United States, a study that examined twenty industrialized countries from 1965 to 2003 shows men's contribution to family work rose from less than one-fifth in 1965 to more than one-third by 2003. The American Time Use Survey gathers more detailed data on how people spend their hours, including how long people spend decorating their homes (inside and out), cleaning up the kitchen, and caring for children and pets. In 2007 it showed that on an average day 83 percent of women and 66 percent of men did something around the house that comprised housework, gardening, or sorting out the family finances. Women spent nearly three hours working away on such household chores, whereas men spent closer to two hours. It won't surprise you that on an average day, 52 percent of women did cleaning or laundry compared to 20 percent of men. Equally predictable is that 64 percent of women versus 37 percent of men did the cooking.

So what happens in lesbian couples, particularly if they have children, which is when most friction around sharing housework occurs? A small study of twenty-nine lesbian couples published in the *Journal of Social and Personal Relationships* found that after couples had children, women still shared their housework quite equally; but the biological mother spent more time on child care. Generally, studies show men increasingly spend more time with their children, but so do women.

So if your man views housework as optional, it's up to you to change his mind. You need to discuss what chores need to be done and which jobs each of you will do. If you have different thresholds for what is dirty and what needs cleaning, you will have to negotiate. You will also need to give him credit for his DIY work. If you continue to feel unappreciated, it will threaten your relationship. But if things get better, don't be tempted to get married. Generally, men who live with someone do more housework than they would if they got married.

Nag or Negotiate?

I feel as though I'm nagging my partner all the time. I am forever saying, "Will you take out the trash?" or "Do you think you could make lunch for the kids for a change?" I'm sure he thinks I'm a nag, and it doesn't work as he "forgets." How can I get him to do things without nagging?

Nagging doesn't work, as you've discovered, and what's more, it's rather unattractive. Nagging, for those who don't do it, is asking someone to do something repeatedly in many different ways, sometimes using different voices (which sound increasingly exasperated). By virtue of having to ask over and over again, nagging is not effective and makes the recipient angry and defensive. This is not to say that the request you originally made is not valid. But relationship experts suggest saying five positive things to your partner for every one negative thing in order to nurture a satisfying relationship, and nagging makes this goal rather difficult.

It's usually women who are accused of nagging, not men. Is this fair? A study, by researchers at the University of Florida and published in the *Journal of Pragmatics*, asked college students to collect examples of nagging during Thanksgiving—a family occasion for which nagging was invented. Out of seventy examples of nagging, women were reported to have done two-thirds of the nagging, and it was mostly over their partner doing (or not doing) a wide range of housework tasks. In the remaining third of the nagging examples (done by men), there were only six examples of the types of things men nagged about, mostly nondomestic issues such as slamming the car door. The researchers suggested that women might have more to nag about.

Nagging is an example of what psychologists call "demand-withdraw behavior." When something matters to only one person, the other one ignores it. How this works is shown in a study of fifty married couples published in the *Journal of Marriage and Family*. Researchers videotaped the couples' discussions of the five most important changes their spouse could make in their behavior that would improve their relationship. The more spouses had to lose by changing their behavior, the more they withdrew from the discussion. And this led to nagging. Put simply, your partner ignores requests to take out the trash because he can't be bothered to get up and carry a smelly trash can down the path. Did you know that already?

No one would suggest that withdrawing is good behavior, but it may be easier to work around it than you think. A study published in the *Journal of Experimental Social Psychology* by a professor who wanted to understand why her husband did the opposite of what she wanted him to do showed that people often do so unconsciously. It is human nature for some people to avoid doing what someone else wants them to do, in order to retain their autonomy. Confronting a psychological imperative head on may be frustrating for both of you.

You could try to rephrase your requests or focus on the bigger issue of negotiating how you share household chores. Stay calm and discuss the nagging. Communicate clearly how you feel about how much you both do around the house. The discussion should work better if you can make your requests in a positive way, for example, "I would really appreciate it if you could take out the trash, as it's the one thing I hate doing." Avoid being accusatory and getting angry. If you hear yourself saying, "You never think of doing"—well, just about anything really—then the discussion is going badly. If nothing works, you may have more fundamental problems. Let's hope you don't; they certainly won't be solved by nagging.

Who Complains More?

> I've just come back from a weekend with my girl-friends, and those of us with relationships spent a lot of time talking about the problems we have with our men. I know that my boyfriend's friends on their guys' weekend away didn't spend time talking about their relationships. Do women complain more about their relationships than men do, and if so, why?

Of course women complain more about their relationships to their friends than men do. The research shows that women not only complain about more problems but also feel lonelier when they're in relationships (they're programmed for intimacy) and are more likely to leave. Figures from the UK Office for National Statistics show that two-thirds of divorces are initiated by women, most of whom cite their husband's unreasonable behavior, a category that could include failing to meet expectations. Men, on the other hand, divorce most often on the more unimaginative or less judgmental grounds that they've been separated for two years. Generally, men seem to be easier to please.

To complain so much, women must have clear ideas of what they want in relationships and thus be able to pinpoint exactly when and how their men fall short of expectations. But do women want from their relationships things that are different from what men want? The journal *Personal Relationships* published a study that asked 122 people who had been in relationships for an average of eleven years (they were between the ages of twenty-three and fifty-nine) to rate the importance of thirty standards for relationships. The standards were obvious stuff: that they and their partner showed they liked each other, talked to each other (about feelings, not just the electricity bill), and were faithful. The study found that men and women agreed on the relative importance of each standard, but that women felt their standards were met less often than men did. Since a lot of the standards were about communication and intimacy, traditionally female strengths, women were bound to do better with them.

Even when men did feel their standards weren't being met, they were less bothered by this than women were. Women are just more aware of how their relationships are doing. Other studies have found that women monitor how their relationships are going more closely than men do. They are therefore more likely than men to notice if the relationship falls short and can feel aggrieved by it.

Psychologists (of both sexes) would argue that women aren't moaning about their relationships; they are "working on them." Men (in psychology studies at least) will say their friendships are "activity" based: they talk more to other men about the state of their sports team than the state of their romantic relationships. Women are more likely to confide in their close friends about practically everything, in detail that may be finer than their men would like. There's good evidence that when women talk about their relationships, they feel supported by doing so. This may be because such conversations help them talk through the problems they have with their partners or because friendships provide some of the intimacy missing from their relationship. Friends may support the relationship rather then denigrate it, particularly if they like the partner. But of course the real reason women complain about their relationships is that there's nothing to say about them (and none of their friends would be interested) when they're going well.

One Too Many?

> My husband and I are in our late sixties and have a good marriage. However, my husband is drinking more these days. He'll have a bottle of wine on the go before midday and drink two to three bottles a day (hiding his glass), but if I mention his drinking he says, "So what? I'm not working anymore." Our relationship has deteriorated—drinking makes him argumentative. He says it isn't a problem, but I think it is. What can I do?

It seems that quite a few older people are drinking more alcohol than is good for them. Physicians are noticing an increase in the phenomenon of men like your husband who spend their retirement catching up on their alcohol consumption rather than on more socially useful activities. They are a rather hidden group, however, as instead of throwing up in the city center on a Saturday night they drink excessively in the privacy of their own homes. A community-based study published in the *International Journal of Addictions* found that around 2 to 4 percent of older people were in the alcoholic bracket.

According to a 2006 article published in the *British Journal of Psychiatry*, older people are one of the groups least informed about alcohol units, and this may be part of the problem. And should anyone be able to remember them, the recommended drinking levels may not be as applicable for older people because age and some medications reduce the ability to metabolize alcohol. Physicians in the United States advise older people to consume no more than one drink a day. This advice, while clear-cut, is thought by many European doctors to be so restrictive as to be draconian.

Alcohol makes people defensive (as well as offensive), so your husband is unlikely to admit to drinking too much. (People who drink too much don't usually admit it, because they associate an alcohol problem with homeless drunks swigging six-packs, not with respectable folk like themselves sipping good wine.) How much is too much is hard to pinpoint unless you're following the U.S. government's dietary guidelines—and most people don't even know them. The Department of Health and Human Services and the Department of Agriculture say moderate drinking is up to one drink for women and two for men per day, and a drink is defined as five fluid ounces of wine, twelve fluid ounces of beer, or one and a half fluid ounces of spirits. The guidelines advise that drinking more than this is not good for your health. But in your husband's case, there's no need to count units; drinking two to three bottles of wine a day is definitely too much. Perhaps most important, do you have any idea why your husband is drinking more? Is it just because he can, or does he, in retirement, feel depressed or lonely? Retirement takes some adjustment. There may have been another stressful event that triggered his drinking problem.

Research into relationships where one partner drinks heavily shows they're unhappy and fraught with arguments, usually about how much the partner is drinking. There's always the risk that fights can get violent. These days, doctors are more aware of the dangers of drinking, and some offer brief interventions that aim to reduce the amount people drink; such interventions involve a few educational sessions about safe limits and the use of alcohol diaries (to document intake rather than to record drunken moments). Older people can usually be helped to drink within the limits again. But for a brief intervention to work, the person has to have some insight into the fact that they have a problem—they may have fallen over when drunk or been caught driving under the influence. There is also the Alcoholics Anonymous option. AA has a sister fellowship called Al-Anon for people like yourself whose lives are affected by others' drinking. You may want to start with Al-Anon, as your husband is unlikely to skip into an AA meeting if he is in denial. Tell him you are going because you are worried about his drinking and suggest he gets some help himself. What isn't an option is to spend your retirement with a partner who's permanently plastered.

"We" Time

My boyfriend and I have busy jobs, and although we live together we rarely spend any quality time in each other's company. He says it doesn't matter; it's just a phase—our work is demanding—and it will pass. I don't think other couples live like that. How much time do most people spend together, and does it matter?

Couples spend much less time together than you'd think. Many couples do feel the strain of working long hours. The UK Office for National Statistics' regular time-use surveys—the sort that tells you useless facts like how many years you spend cutting your toenails—have found our time is mostly divided between sleep, work, and watching television. On average couples spend two to two and a half hours a day with their significant others, including on weekends. Add in children, and just over one of those hours disappears into rearranging plastic dinosaurs. And what do couples do when they're alone with their loved ones? Watch television (one-third of all the time spent together), eat (thirty minutes), and do housework together (twenty-four minutes). Whoopee. Married people spend half an hour more together than people who cohabit. (The mystery is how retired couples spend only four hours a day together. Are they avoiding each other?)

In the United States, the closest look at time spent together comes from a paper presented in 2007 at the American Time Use Resource Conference that divided time spent on activities into an average per day. The data came from diaries kept by couples for the American Time Use Survey and showed that couples spend most of their time together going out to the movies, theater, bars, or restaurants or watching sports events, socializing at home, and watching television. Most time was spent watching television together, but perhaps if that includes snuggling up, it's a good thing.

Dual-earning couples may spend less time together. During congressional testimony on the challenges facing American workers, researchers from the New America Foundation said that working mothers were sacrificing time for themselves and their relationship—spending eight hours less with their spouse per week than women who didn't work.

For many, this lack of time with partners is a problem. An ICM poll of 2,004 adults in 2007 found that 64 percent of men and women cited spending time with their family or finding time for their key relationships as their biggest concern—ahead of money and health. So clearly it worries many people, if not your partner.

By asking your partner for "quality" time, you presumably mean time when you interact. Television can be passive unless you have a lively chat about the shows you've seen. A study from Brigham Young University and Colorado State University tracked the leisure activities and relationships of 318 couples who were married or lived together. They found that women cared more than men about spending time together but were clear that the time had to involve talking to each other. If you can't remember what an activity like that would be, think of visiting a place of interest (an art gallery rather than a bar) or cooking together. Whatever you do together as a couple, you need to talk to each other either during or after the activity to make it a communal activity. Just being with your partner doesn't make your relationship better.

So of course it matters if you don't spend much time together or if that time is spent having a TV dinner or working on adjacent laptops. A study published in the *Journal of Sex Research* of 6,029 couples from the U.S. National Survey of Families and Households found (somewhat obviously) that the less time couples spent together, the less sex they had. It's worse if you or your partner feels overwhelmed by work. A study from Penn State University studied the quality of the relationships that 190 men had with their wives and their teenage children. It turns out that couples are much happier when they've agreed on the longer hours (perhaps to afford a move to a new house) than when they haven't.

Don't just hope that things will get better. Phases have a tendency to develop into the natural order of things. Suggest that you spend at least one evening a week together, either at home but talking to each other, or on a "date." The survey by the UK Office for National Statistics suggests that if you don't make time for each other, you'll have a whole relationship, not just a phase, that's based on sleeping and television.

Income-linked Divorce

> My wife earns more than I do. This was true when I met her, and it's never bothered me. Since we've had children, I have done more child care and housework than she has. I read somewhere that couples have a 50 percent higher divorce rate when the wife is the higher earner than when the husband earns more. Is this true?

The number of women working and the amount they earn has gone up (although men still earn on average 23.5 percent more than women according to the U.S. Census Bureau).

Women who are the main breadwinners are still a minority. Most women in this category are not high-flying bankers but low earners whose partners make even less or are unemployed. The research is inconclusive. One study found that for every five-thousand-dollar increase in a wife's annual income, the odds of divorce increased by 5 percent. Other studies show that a wife's earnings reduce the risk of divorce because with two incomes the couple's lives are more comfortable and they have more to lose financially by splitting up. Many couples need two incomes to maintain their standard of living. A paper by Stephen Sweet of Ithaca College published in the journal *Research in the Sociology of Work* reported that dual-income families were the norm for a reasonable standard of living and that many families had no savings and relied on two incomes.

The old-fashioned concerns around a wife earning more than her husband are that it's unnatural and will turn him into a resentful, inadequate wet blanket and that a wife who earns more will leave at the slightest excuse because she can afford to. Economic dependency has traditionally been thought to make women more committed to their marriages. However, attitudes have changed. A survey by the dating Web site True .com, which has 2.7 million users, found that a third of their male users (no numbers were given) actually wanted women who earned more than they did.

Most of the studies citing higher divorce rates are old and flawed, because they used individuals instead of couples and so couldn't find out if divorces were due to one person holding traditional views about a man's income and status, or the fact that the wife brought home the larger slice of bacon. How much importance men and women attach to work is clearly significant. One of the more thorough studies, of a randomized group of 286 dual-earning couples that was published in the *Journal of Marriage and Family*, found that only men who felt defined by their salary became upset if their wives earned more. Which is still a lot of men. The study showed that women didn't mind earning more, and since they don't have the historical baggage of linking self-worth to salary they don't care if they earn less either. What made them happy in relationships were husbands, like you, who did their share of child care and housework.

Another study, using the National Survey of Families and

Testing Times

Households, which includes over five thousand American couples, found that both men and women were happier when the husband was the major breadwinner (and this study is only a few years old). But the single most important factor in deciding how happy a woman was in her marriage had nothing to do with income. Above all, they wanted men who were emotionally involved. The latter being something that money can't buy.

Outlaw the In-laws?

> My mother-in-law is critical of me and makes snide comments. My husband doesn't seem to notice but gets upset if I get upset. Since we have had our son, who is two, her behavior has gotten worse and she visits more often. We got along better before the marriage. Should I ban her from the house, have it out with her, or rise above it?

These are all fair options if your mother-in law is criticizing you. Unfortunately, while there's research on strife with the mother-in-law (and tons of feeble jokes), there aren't any studies on what to do about it. There are Web sites such as the Secret Society of Tortured Daughters-in-Law (www.tortureddaughtersinlaw.com) and one that advertises help for Parents-in-Law Phobia (www.changethatsrightnow.com) and offers a therapy program. Essentially they'd probably support a ban (provided your husband is willing).

You both love the same man, and that doesn't usually work. You understand mother love yourself now—how fierce and unconditional it is. Imagine your son grown up with a girlfriend or wife and how you would watch and possibly judge her. This isn't to excuse your mother-in-law's behavior, but it's worth understanding it. How sure can you be that when you're a mother-in-law you'll do any better?

As you begin bringing up your young family, your mother-in-law has finished that phase of her life. Ideally, she should maintain a limited interest in yours and be involved when you ask her rather than as she sees fit. But your negative relationship with her will infect your marriage. A study of the influence of in-laws on the success of marriages by researchers at Iowa State University found that couples were more likely to break up when the wife and mother-in-law didn't get along than when there wasn't conflict. Out of the 403 husbands in the study, 33 got divorced over four years, and conflict between wives and mothers-in-law had a significantly negative effect on the marriages. Other studies show that once a couple has children, this is often a source of tension with mothers-in-law, who believe they know best about all aspects of child rearing.

A team from the University of Arkansas interviewed twenty-three daughters-in-law and nineteen mothers-in-law. It found that tensions arose from the slightest things. Wives didn't like their mothers-in-law leaving phone messages only for their husband. Mothers-in-law felt hurt when their daughters-in-law didn't rush to greet them at social events. The relationship often deteriorated over wedding plans and imagined slights.

Mothers-in-law are less judgmental about their daughters-in-law than vice versa (all the studies show this) and are often mystified as to how they have offended them. Getting to know your mother-in-law as a woman in her own right outside of polite family gatherings may make it easier for both of you to tolerate each other. So, before you ban her, get to know her a bit better.

Be kind to her and have a talk with your husband about how she makes you feel. Remember not to call her anything that will upset him, because that witch is his mother. Ask him for ideas on how to deal with her criticism and present a united front if you need to confront her about it. Fortunately, though, there is good research that suggests that too much contact with the in-laws causes trouble, so you shouldn't see too much of her—as if you didn't know that already.

Pathetic Presents

> I love Christmas, and I work hard to make it special for the family. But my partner's presents to me are so disappointing. He's lovely and we get along well, but his presents are so functional and unromantic that I feel hurt by them. One year he got me a cell phone charger. I get upset that he either doesn't know me at all or doesn't care enough. Shall I tell him what to buy me—though it takes the fun out of it?

Does telling your man what to buy you for Christmas take the fun out of it? Well, it's not much fun now, is it? The easiest option is to direct him to a survey—such as one from Pricegrabber.com, which has 21 million users a month—showing that the top gifts women want are jewelry and clothing. Cell phone chargers don't make the list; neither do foot spa machines and cordless irons. An overwhelming 1 percent of women said they wanted a do-it-yourself tool. Men (in case you're interested) want the latest electronic gizmo, often a television. They are also more likely to assume that women, like them, want something useful.

Most surveys show that women put more effort into and spend more money at Christmas. Dr. Anne Wilson, a social psychologist at Wilfrid Laurier University in Canada, says that women think of gifts as communicating emotional purpose more than men do. Men will be happy with a DIY gadget because . . . hey, tools are useful. But does your partner's present mean he doesn't know you? Wilson says that too often we make assumptions that our partners know us better than they actually do. The notion that people close to you can read you like an open book is just wrong, particularly at Christmas.

You suggest his useless present-buying has even deeper meaning—that it reflects how (little) he feels about you. This is unlikely to be true and is rather unfair to him. In fact, your response says more about you than his gift. Research shows that women spend more time than men judging how responsive their partner is. Men assume (forgive the generalizations) that if they're happy, so is their partner. In a study led by Dr. Sandra Murray from the State University of New York at Buffalo, 173 couples kept a daily diary of how they got along (measured by psychological scoring systems). Lots of them felt occasionally hurt by their partner, but those who felt confident about themselves responded by trying to get closer to their partner. Those who didn't behaved in ways guaranteed to push their partner away by being distant or moody. Most of the people who felt undervalued underestimated how much their partners cared about them and how happy their partners were in the relationship. In fact, the people who agonized over why their partners stayed with them were loved just as much as others who felt more secure. So check your self-esteem, tell him exactly what you want for Christmas, and, in the interests of getting closer, go and buy him the latest TV. If you can't afford that, try a nice drill instead.

Question of Misery

I had a miscarriage two months ago. I was only about six weeks pregnant and have two small

children, and although I felt sad, I was almost re-
lieved. However, my partner still seems upset, and
we are now quite distant from each other. Is this rift
normal, and will it get better? I feel a bit upset that
he's miserable when I'm the one who had the miscarriage.

You alone had the miscarriage, but both of you would have
been parents to the baby. Around one in four pregnancies end
in miscarriage, and even when it occurs early on, it's unsettling and distressing, however ambivalent you feel about the
pregnancy. And like many difficulties in relationships, it's as
likely to pull you apart as push you together. A study published in the *Journal of Perinatology* shows that 85 percent of
couples share their feelings about miscarriage in a limited way,
if at all. Men worry so much about saying the wrong thing
that—guess what?—they may say nothing at all.

Traditionally there's been less attention paid to the reac-
tion of men after miscarriages because the physical effects of
a miscarriage belong exclusively to the woman. But a study in
the journal *Evolutionary Psychology* asked over three hundred
men in the north of England how they felt after their partner's
miscarriage. Compared with women's reactions, these men
were less acutely distressed, though they had more difficulty
coping long-term. Some of the men reported feeling grief and
despair. Men will have felt the baby to be less real than their
partner during the pregnancy but still feel the loss at the
miscarriage—especially if they have seen the baby on an ultra-
sound scan. The men in the study also said they were worried
about their partner's health and feelings. Other studies show
that men can feel a range of emotions (including nothing)
such as empathy, powerlessness, fear of the future, and sometimes resentment about the whole business.

So this is why your partner feels upset. But why are you feeling frustrated? Feeling angry after a miscarriage is common, as is depression and anxiety. When we feel sad, it's normal, if unattractive, to take it out on those dearest to us. But maybe you feel your partner is so busy being sad that he isn't supporting you. A study of 185 women led by Kristen Swanson, a professor of family and child nursing, and researchers from the University of Washington found that one year after miscarriage, one-third of couples were more distant, avoiding sex and feeling tense with each other. This was more likely to happen when women couldn't discuss their loss with their partner and felt unloved and unsupported. Women are more likely to feel depressed and angry if their partner won't talk about the miscarriage and better able to cope when their partner shows he cares—preferably by making a fuss over them.

It's normal for the two of you to have reacted differently. Women feel better about miscarriages when they share their feelings; men often feel they are treading on eggshells when they do so. What you must do is be kind and patient with each other and talk about what's happened, accepting that your reactions won't be the same. It will be worth the effort. Swanson's study found that the other two-thirds of couples said their relationships after miscarriage were either as good as they had been before or even closer and happier.

Having Your Cake

I've been in a relationship for six years but recently met this man when our children played together in the park. He's a single parent, and we've met a few times with the children and once on our own. I'm completely blown away by him. I think I'm in love and want to be with him, but I really love my boyfriend. Can you be in love with two people at the same time?

You might think there's no research to answer your question (which is as much philosophical as psychological), and you'd be right. How can you know if you're in love with him? An on-line survey of over 1,100 readers of *Psychology Today* (many of whom are psychologists) found that two-thirds thought you could be in love with more than one person at once. Support comes from parental love (which embraces more than one child), and if you don't buy that because it's asexual, there are some polygamous love marriages (and polygamy has strict rules to avoid favoritism). Most people have friends who feel that they have been in love with two people at once. But once you start sleeping with two people, this is called infidelity, which sounds far less lofty.

Psychologists have tried to measure styles of loving by using such devices as the Love Attitude Scale. At the heart of these, aside from passion and intensity, are the attributes of friendship, dependency, altruism, and commitment. Is it possible to be altruistic and committed to two men? Is it possible to feel that much for someone you don't know that well? The Passion-ate Love Scale—where love is defined as an intense longing to be with someone—asks how preoccupied you are when think-ing about them, and how much you want to please and be with them. This scale has equal amounts of pain and pleasure. But any scale has only limited value—for researchers rather than individuals. No scales can package love as a block of mea-surable science; there's emotion and compulsion in love.

Another type of measurable love, companionate love, is defined by psychologists as the more committed type of love, based on having lives that are strongly intertwined. Ideally, relationships have both. What often happens is that companionate love loses enough of its passion to make other people, who have that edginess of attraction, more appealing.

One important point to bear in mind: psychologists say that you're unlikely to be in love with two people at the same time who are similar. Your boyfriend may be pragmatic, your new love a poet. Some also say (brace yourself) that healthy people are satisfied in a relationship with one person and only narcissists and people with dysfunctional emotional lives think they can be in love with two people at the same time. Sorry about that.

Your existing relationship is likely to win out because there's more invested in it, unless you proceed to have an affair, which will seriously damage your existing relationship. Stop seeing this new man and improve the relationship with your old one. Breathe back into it some of the life that may have been extinguished by children and familiarity. Some people may advise you to go for this new love (although it seems speculative to call it love just yet) because your happiness is the most important thing. But that would be tough on your and his children and also on your boyfriend. It's analogous to driving a comfortable, steady Ford and seeing a shiny Porsche that makes your heart race again. Choosing a newer model may or may not be the right choice, but it would certainly be the most costly for everyone concerned.

10

Happily Ever After

Not Just a Film

> We've been married for seven years this October.
> We have a daughter who's three, and we get along
> pretty well compared to other couples we know. But
> I wonder if there's really such a thing as the seven-
> year itch, and if so, what can you do to prevent it?

The idea of a seven-year itch comes from the film of that
name starring Marilyn Monroe, who looked rather tempting
when her dress was blown upward by a subway vent. In real
life, the UK Office for National Statistics says that 19 percent
of divorces happen within the first four years, 27 percent between five and nine years, and 13 percent between fifteen and
nineteen years. The median length of marriage in England is
now around seven years for women marrying between the ages
of twenty-five and thirty-four. In the United States, according

to Larry Bumpass, a professor at the University of Wisconsin, one-half of marriages end within seven years. Couples who live together start scratching earlier; John Ermisch from the University of Essex in England says that for women in their thirties the median time they live with a romantic partner is three and a half years.

The seven-year itch reflects couples' disillusionment with each other more than some couples' search for alternatives. (The basis for most divorces is incompatibility, irreconcilable differences, or the irremediable breakdown of the marriage, all available under the no-fault divorce option offered by most states.) Generally, the honeymoon period is over quickly. It used to be cute that he ate cold beans from the can; now it's disgusting. There's a deafening sound of scales falling from eyes within the first four years. Many studies have looked at this potentially depressing phenomenon, such as the one carried out over a period of eight years by Lawrence Kurdek and published in *Developmental Psychology*. Kurdek compared the answers from 538 couples (one of the problems is that only 93 couples were left by the end of the study—and maybe they were the unhappiest) to over thirty questions, such as how affectionate and dependable their significant others were and how much they agreed on important issues. He also asked about "dysfunctional beliefs," so listen up, as they include thinking that arguing is bad (it's how you argue that counts), that sex should be perfect, and that your partner should intuitively understand you. He found a clear dip in happiness after four years and another around eight years when the couples were questioned again, particularly for couples with children and those previously divorced. Not surprisingly, he advises couples to modify their expectations. Prepare, in fact, for disappointment, because it is likely to happen.

Research by John M. Gottman, one of the best-known

relationship researchers in the United States, shows that it's possible to predict with 94 percent accuracy which couples will divorce, even before they marry, after watching them talk for a few minutes on a thorny issue. Couples who say five positive things to one negative are likely to survive. Below that, they're in trouble. Gottman has also studied gay and lesbian couples, and in a study published in the *Journal of Homosexuality* he reported that these couples are less belligerent, fairer, and more considerate to each other. They were generally better at resolving arguments. In heterosexual relationships, if the man listens to the woman in a dispute (really, I'm not making this up), if they can avoid sneering at each other (contempt, says Gottman, is sulfuric acid for relationships), criticizing, or withdrawing (what tactics are you left with then?), it may make for a terribly dull argument, but it reduces the risk of scratching after seven years.

Leaving the Nest

> My daughter goes off to college this year. My son moved out two years ago. My husband and I will soon be on our own together. Although we get along pretty well, I really dread her leaving. I've heard of couples splitting up after twenty years of marriage once their children left home. What usually happens to couples when their children leave home?

The risk of empty-nest syndrome (depression and loss of purpose after your children have left home) has been rather exaggerated. Mothers used to be prescribed antidepressants by their family doctor before their children had shut the door behind them. But most mothers are actually happier once their children move out. That psychological umbilical cord may be strong, but a mother's (and father's) job is to cut it and launch their children into independent adult lives. That your kids will never be able to afford a mortgage unless you can cough up the deposit is a small detail.

Mothers undoubtedly do miss their children, but they get over it. A study of 318 mothers by researchers at the Battelle Human Affairs Research Center in Seattle measured their psychological well-being before and after their youngest child had left home. The study found that after six months to a year (well, you'll miss them initially) most women felt much happier once their children had moved out. They were only upset if their children were not coping in the outside world. A similar and more recent study by researchers from the University of Melbourne in Australia of 438 women also found that mothers reported fewer daily hassles and that they felt better when their children left home—but only if they weren't worrying about them.

So do happy mothers mean happier marriages? (The research is not clear on how fathers feel, but traditionally they are thought to be less upset.) Some experts, such as Dr. Karen Fingerman, associate professor of developmental and family studies at the University of Michigan, have said that most parents enjoy "reconnecting" with their spouses and also get along better with their children once they've left home. They also, if they put their minds to it, have a great time. A survey of 1,190 parents by the international insurance firm Zurich shows that 42 percent of empty nesters take more vacations together and 36 percent spend more quality time (including having sex again) with their partner. Are you still dreading your daughter's departure?

With the children gone, there is the fear that your relationship will be exposed as past its sell-by date—that you'll have nothing left to talk about. The research is inconclusive on whether empty nesters are more likely to divorce. Some couples do delay leaving unhappy marriages until their children grow up, but there is some research that shows marriages grow stronger as the stress of having children around disappears, and longer marriages are also stronger because they have more invested in them. That said, one U.S. study did find that for couples married twenty years, an empty nest increased their chances of divorce, but for those married twenty-eight years or more it reduced it. Doing things together and talking (nicely) to each other also improve your chances of staying together. So you should enjoy yourselves and start spending your children's inheritance before they finish college and move back in again.

Relationship Recovery

My partner was laid off from his job five months ago. Thanks to my job, we're okay financially, and he is trying to find work, but he's moody—there's no affection or sex. If his attitude doesn't improve, he'll lose me as well as his job. How much of this is inevitable with a layoff? Can I make things better?

It's not hard to imagine what it feels like to lose your job, income, structure to your day, and the answer to "What do you do?" The reality is probably ten times as bad. So your partner is moody? Lost his libido? Perfectly normal. Be thankful he's not suffered anything worse. A study published in the *British Medical Journal* of 6,191 men between the ages of forty and fifty-nine found that those who lost their jobs during the five years of the study were twice as likely to die as those who didn't. When social class, smoking, drinking, and existing health problems were taken into account, the risk of dying fell, but only slightly. These men had had steady employment for the five years before the study and so were normal, healthy working folk. However, relax: this isn't to say a layoff kills you—it's only an association. What downsizing does do for many people is take away their reason for getting up in the morning.

Other studies show that being laid off causes depression (not an unsurprising finding) and a tendency to drink more alcohol than is good for you. There is some evidence that it can increase the risk of suicide. But it partly depends on the circumstances of being laid off. If it happens through a massive downsizing or when unemployment is high, it's less damaging to couples because it doesn't reflect on the person being laid off. It's got nothing to do with them—it's the economy, stupid. There is some evidence that layoff makes a marriage more precarious. A study by researchers at the Institute of Social and Economic Research using a large Swedish data set found that a job loss increased the risk of divorce by 18 percent in the first year. This was true whether it was men or women who lost their jobs. The author speculates that it's not the job loss itself or financial issues (he cites generous welfare benefits in Sweden), but something more subtle that erodes relationships. For example, laid-off people may feel that their partners can't understand them and find them less attractive.

Couples who can cope financially and get support from friends and family are more likely to stay together after a layoff. So get some help. Enlist your partner's friends to take him out. Talk to him kindly. Say you want to be with him, but he seems unhappy and distant. Could he reconsider this approach to being laid off? Be affectionate and make it clear you find him attractive. Encourage him to use his time to sort things

203

out in the house (every house needs some sorting out) and re-assure him that he is more likely than not to find another job, but it may take some time. Tell him that while you understand how tough this situation is and how much he is struggling, you miss the "old him." To you, the job he used to have was never the most important thing about him.

Sofa So Good?

> My partner says we need to have counseling for our relationship. I agree with her that we've grown apart: we argue a lot and rarely have sex or spend any quality time together. I'm committed to this relation-ship (we have two children), but can counseling save our relationship, or has she already made up her mind to leave?

Relationship counseling can save relationships, but only if a couple want it to. Surveys suggest that only 9 to 23 percent of people use counseling to get out of a relationship. One of the problems is that few couples use it at all. Only 20 percent of divorced people tried relationship counseling before seeing a lawyer. By the time couples get to counseling their relation-ships are often in their death throes; studies show many of those lining up for outside help score highly on scales of dis-tress (that is, they are very unhappy indeed).

There's a lot of research showing that therapy improves relationships. The couples-counseling service Relate's own surveys say that 58 percent of its clients believe their relation-ships improved after counseling, and 80 percent are satisfied with the therapy they are given. A detailed report from AC-CORD, an Irish Catholic "marriage care service" that both analyzed existing research and included its own study of 1,500 couples and 1,000 individuals, also claimed success for counseling. It found that half of the men and women in its study were less stressed after counseling and that a quarter improved their behavior: they were less critical, argued less, and listened more. (Not listening was especially an issue for men; women are more likely to criticize their partner.) This sample, however, may be biased, because ACCORD is a Catholic organization with couples who may be more motivated to save their marriages.

More research comes from the highly experienced John Simons, whose review paper for the Lord Chancellor's Department of the United Kingdom is rather less optimistic. He points out that while therapy works (and the many different types have the same effects) in studies, it is less effective in real life. In research studies it is not uncommon, because the conditions are not exactly the same as in usual practice (for example, depressed couples may be excluded from the study to make it easier to analyze results), to find that the positive effects of treatments are inflated. Simons says that half of all couples are still distressed after six to eight therapy sessions. There's also a high relapse rate; couples revert to insults and not listening to each other after a few months of good behavior. He cites the work of John M. Gottman, who says that relationship counseling has a limited effect: after two years, it improves relationships only by 11 to 18 percent.

Couples who come to counseling and really want to make their relationships work do better than those in less committed relationships. An Australian survey of 1,302 people in the late 1980s found that out of those who wanted to stay in a relationship, 73 percent of women and 66 percent of men had done so. Interestingly, 25 percent of men and 38 percent of women who said they wanted to leave also remained. Couples who fared the worst showed little affection, rarely had sex, and didn't share housework or child-care responsibilities.

So your partner is probably genuinely trying to improve your relationship, and counseling may well help to do that. You've got a lot at stake here. Given what you have to lose, how hard can it be to be less insulting and critical, to do more housework, to listen more, and to be more affectionate? And it's so much better for the whole family.

Remarriage Rush

> My mother died five months ago from cancer. My father, who's sixty-eight, was inconsolable but is now seeing my mother's best friend, who's divorced. I'm his youngest daughter and want him to be happy, but isn't he a bit heartless to be dating so quickly?

It's usually *because* widowers miss their wives so much that they look for companionship with someone else so quickly. Men often react differently than women do when their partner dies. There's the myth that says women mourn for and men replace their partners. Except it's not completely a myth, because the numbers say that widowers are at least one and a half times more likely to remarry than widows.

There are various reasons why widows are less likely to remarry—there are fewer older men, for a start. But there are more subtle factors at work. A study of twenty-five widows and twenty-six widowers over the age of sixty-five, published in the journal *Ageing International*, found that women mourned for longer periods of time. Both men and women didn't like feeling lonely and wanted someone to take out for supper and go on vacation with, but women preferred dating to remarriage. The women's reasons were similar: they'd had one happy marriage, their spouses were irreplaceable, and they didn't want to look after another man.

Men were more eager to fill the vacant position of wife and companion. Your dad just wants someone to do the things that your mother did. You may wonder if that includes sex—it does sometimes, and increasingly so now that there are drugs that can help on that front. But these older, postbereavement relationships are more about support than passion. Even so, the same success factors for relationships apply; widowers who are healthy and financially better off are more likely to meet someone else.

The need that widowers have for support is confirmed by a study of 35 widowers and 215 widows from researchers at the University of New Brunswick in Canada, published in the *Journal of Marriage and Family*. Six months after the death, about 15 percent of men were dating, compared to less than 1 percent of women, and 30 percent of men wanted to remarry; for women it was 16 percent. Widows got emotional support and help from friends and their children, while the widowers, in contrast, got much less. Your dad, like the widowers in this study, is looking less for someone to make the supper and more for the woman to share it with. It is the ache left by the loss of their main emotional confidante that they want to fill. Widows in this study were more likely to want someone to "go out with" than someone to "go home to."

The study found that widowers with the same emotional support from friends and family as widows shared the same reduced level of need for future relationships. So it might also be that your dad is simply lonely, despite your love and support. Please don't disapprove of his dating; bereaved children can and do wreck these relationships. A study in the *Annals of*

Clinical Psychiatry found that men and women who were dating or had remarried two years after being widowed were happier than those who weren't. Most people would want that for their fathers.

Menopausal Madness

> I am nearing the age of menopause, and I am dreading it. I expect to dry up, go off sex, and find that my husband has left me for someone younger. I am being serious, as this has happened to women I know. Can I do anything to stop it from happening?

It's no longer politically correct to suggest that the menopause is a terrible condition for women. Didn't you know that? It's part of our life cycle, although inconveniently it comes rather early, leaving women without lubrication for at least a third of their lives. It was once thought to make women sad and stupid. In the 1960s a paper published in the *Journal of the American Geriatric Society* talked about menopausal women acquiring "a vapid cow-like feeling called a negative state."

Menopause is defined as not having menstruated for a year and usually occurs around the age of fifty, but it is preceded by a few years of hormones winding down. It's hard to see any positive effects from losing estrogen; negative effects include mood swings, an increased risk of heart disease, loss of skin elasticity, dryness in most places except when sweating from a hot flash (72 percent of women), weight gain, and anxiety. Your anxiety seems to be around your husband leaving you. Did I mention low self-esteem, another menopausal side effect? Of course, you no longer have to worry about pregnancy—but will you still be having sex?

Thankfully, the research has some recommendations on how to survive menopause, although it requires a bit of effort. You need to exercise, keep having sex, and avoid putting on too much weight. At the risk of sounding shallow, feeling frumpy is terrible for menopausal women. It stops them from having sex, which is a well-known adhesive for couples. A study by the Midlife Women's Health Survey of 307 American women between the ages of thirty-five and fifty-five found that the less attractive a woman felt, the more likely she was to have gone off sex. Around 57 percent of these women wanted less sex. The study, in the *Journal of Sex Research*, said that body fat doubles by the time women reach fifty, with waists getting thicker and breasts saggier. Oh, great. Men, too, get wider, and also balder, but seem to retain their self-esteem.

Your husband is not likely to run off with someone. In fact, you're more likely to do so. In *The Female Brain*, the psychiatrist Louann Brizendine argues that 65 percent of divorces among people over the age of fifty are initiated by women. She says this may be due to lower estrogen levels making them reassess their relationships (known as waking up and smelling the roses). The most common reason for divorce in the United States is irreconcilable differences, but in the United Kingdom adultery comes a close second to the most common reason (unreasonable behavior). However, more husbands use adultery as the basis for divorce than wives do.

Women vary in how they go through menopause, but most don't get depressed and do cope with the physical symptoms. If you want medical help, it's worth discussing options with your doctor, but menopause doesn't have to be treated as a disease, so first talk to your partner, friends, and family. Or, even better, talk to anyone who's been through it. You're right to think about your relationship, although maybe not so negatively.

Talk to your husband, make sure you have a close, good relationship, and pay attention to your sex life. If everything else was all right before menopause, a drop in estrogen levels won't ruin it.

Keeping Mum

> My mother died six months ago, and I've been hurt by how unsupportive my husband has been. He was kind initially, but now he's irritated by my grief and never asks how I am feeling. We've been together for eight years, but now I wonder if this is what he's really like. How can I get him to be more understanding?

Losing a parent is usually deeply upsetting, but not everyone understands this. Your spouse may assume that as an adult you should shrug your grief off rather quickly. After all, we all know our parents are going to die, don't we? Yet the reality is that the death of any loved one can make you sad and ill and feel unsupported. Studies say that the bereaved commonly complain of "a difficulty getting along with people." Combine this with findings from other studies that document how adversity of any kind tends to make relationships unhappier, and you can see the inevitability about your dissatisfaction. This is a shame, because one of the things you want from a partner is reliable support when things get tough.

Most research on what the loss of a parent does to relationships comes from the United States. Debra Umberson, a psychologist at the University of Texas, surveyed 802 people (123 bereaved and 679 nonbereaved for comparison), asking about support and "harmony" in their relationship. In her study, published in the *Journal of Marriage and Family*, she asked how strongly people agreed with a number of statements such as, "There have been things that have happened in our relationship that I can never forgive." The death of a mother made spouses less supportive and relationships more unhappy (as did the death of a father). These effects were more pronounced in financially better off and more educated couples. The researcher suggests these couples may have been protected from nasty things and so the bereavement is more disruptive.

Umberson went on to interview seventy-three adults in depth and found general disappointment in how quickly partners expected a return to "business-as-usual" and felt inconvenienced by their partner's tears and disinclination to have sex. This sample was recruited from a notice in a newspaper and is likely to be biased, in that the people who volunteered to talk to a researcher may have been more distressed by either their loss or their spouse's response. Certain themes, however, are supported by other research, such as a partner just not getting how it felt to lose a parent.

So it's most likely that your partner is simply underperforming as expected. Or it may be that he has never been that great at talking to you, and your mother's death just makes it glaringly obvious. Some people are less empathic by nature than others; you need to suggest to your partner how he can help you and your relationship. Tell him that you'll feel sad for a while and to bear with you, preferably with kindness. Losing a parent often makes siblings closer, so maybe you can find support elsewhere. Umberson also found that the most understanding partners had themselves lost a parent. So your partner will have the benefit of your experience when the same thing happens to him.

Many Happy Retirements

My wife is retiring in a few months, and I'm worried that when she stops working she'll be lost. She's always worked full-time, even after we had children. She's hinting that I could retire too (although I wouldn't get a pension yet). I don't know any retired couples—is retirement difficult to get used to? We used to joke about longing for retirement, but it doesn't seem so funny now.

People generally have mixed feelings about retiring. Psychologists say it's a time of transition that continues for months after the multiple send-offs, with their presents (often related to a hobby) and embarrassing speeches. When you retire, you lose your job, the money that goes with it, and the routine that finds you crushed on a commuter train each morning. Traditionally, men suffered more than women when they retired, but more recent research (cited by the Policy Studies Institute in the United Kingdom) suggests it can hurt women more, because with career breaks for children they believe they could have achieved more in their working lives.

The Policy Studies Institute (in its own study) asked forty-eight men and women how they'd coped with retirement and found the happiest people were those in couples who had strong ideas about what they wanted to do and saw retirement as an opportunity to see friends and develop interests. Having enough money and being in good health increased the chances of a happy retirement.

In the United States, the Health and Retirement Study (HRS, launched in 1992) reassuringly found that most people are happy and active in retirement. In 2000, 61 percent said they found the "retirement transition" to be "very satisfying" with most of the rest saying they were moderately satisfied and only 7 percent saying they were not satisfied. Again, people who were financially secure were happier to retire and positive reasons for wanting to do so were mostly centered around being able to spend more time with their family. Despite most people saying they would have liked to have retired gradually, most did so abruptly.

The stereotype of retired men getting under the feet of their long-suffering wives may be less common now, but the problem remains. When one and later both of you are at home all day, what does this do to your relationship? The HRS found that most couples decided together who would retire and when they would do so. Ideally, you should have started talking about this five years ago, planning what you'll both do together and apart (playing cards and going on cruises are good activities, but there are many other things you can do, including volunteer work) and how you will pay for it. Of course, if you are leaving a stressful job, you may find that retirement improves your relationship enormously.

Even so, it is likely to take time to settle after retirement. The research shows that although couples eventually make this adjustment, they fight more in the first two years of retiring. A study by researchers at La Trobe University in Australia, using data on over three hundred married people, found that some had a honeymoon period after retirement while others had more troubled times. However, generally the better and worse times evened out after three years, when nearly half the couples said they were happier in retirement. Couples who retire together may find it easier to adjust because they automatically have a companion whose life has changed in the same way. Couples participating in the research of the Policy Studies Institute said that after retiring together they grew closer and happier.

You need to start talking about both of your retirement plans. Immediately would be best. If you don't want to retire yet, be clear about this, as being pushed into it will damage your relationship. Don't worry, your wife will find things to do, but her retiring will take time for both of you to get used to. It's not a single event we're talking about, but the rest of your lives.

Ache of Hearts

> My grandmother died after a short illness, and my grandfather went downhill shortly afterward, with high blood pressure and heart trouble. We think he doesn't want to go on living without her, and although we visit and look after him, he is clearly unhappy and frail. Is it true you can die from a broken heart?

A broken heart is not just a figure of speech; it's a genuine medical emergency. It was the *New England Medical Journal*, not given to flights of fancy, that coined the term "broken heart syndrome." Other medical journals, too, have described cases of people who have died suddenly from heart attacks after traumatic events. It seems that you can either die from a broken heart or from being scared to death; the mechanism is much the same. People usually get chest pain and feel breathless, just as if they're having a heart attack. Something happens to your heart to disrupt the normal beating of its muscle, specifically in the area of the chunky left ventricle (lower left chamber), which pushes blood out around the body. Dr. Ilan S.

Wittstein from Johns Hopkins University School of Medicine estimates that 2 percent of people with heart attack symptoms have broken heart syndrome, which is a lot of sad or frightened people, because heart attacks are fairly common. In a review of the research in this area, nearly 90 percent of broken hearts occurred in women (wouldn't you just know it), particularly in those between fifty-eight and seventy-seven years of age. Maybe your grandfather has a softer heart than most men.

The cause of broken heart syndrome is thought to be a surge in stress hormones such as adrenaline, which stun the heart, although it's not clear how they do this. This is a different scenario from your average heart attack, which is due to blocked arteries cutting off the blood supply to the heart muscle. But the good news is that people recover well; only 3.5 percent will have another attack.

This doesn't mean, however, that the loss of a loved one can't have a lasting, negative impact on your health. A study published in the *British Medical Journal* in 1969 followed up 4,486 widowers ages fifty-five and over and found that 213 died within the first six months of their wife dying, 40 percent above the expected rate for married men of that age. Most died of heart disease (common things being common), but these death rates returned to normal after six months. Another study of 903 relatives of patients dying in a semirural part of Wales found that 4.8 percent died within a year, compared to 0.68 percent of people who hadn't lost a relative. The difference was most profound among widows and widowers, who had ten times the death rate (mostly from heart disease) of people who hadn't lost their spouse. However, once again the physical trauma was relatively short-lived. After the first year the rates returned to normal.

Widowers tend to do worse than widows because they are

more socially isolated and get less support from friends and family. Depression is common in widowers too, and this will make your grandfather less able to look after himself. Try to get him to eat healthily and stay active. The risk of dying from a broken heart may be greatest early on, and if you can get your grandfather through the first difficult year, he may still be sad but physically he'll be in better shape.

Everlasting Love

> I've been with my partner for ten years, and we have two children under ten. Our relationship has gotten less passionate and more routine. What's our relationship going to be like in twenty to thirty years' time? How can we manage to stay together and not be bored with each other?

The path of happiness in relationships follows a U-shaped curve. Happiness falls rapidly in the first years of a relationship, plateaus, and then climbs again, usually once the children leave home. Some research shows the happiness of couples without children follows the same curve. This suggests that couples in the twilight of their years (or sagging middle age) enjoy their relationships as much as they did when they first got together. But are they really having a great time? Or are they saying, "We're stuck with each other; let's make the best of it"?

The ingredients for a happy relationship are well known. John M. Gottman, in his "Love Lab," has analyzed video interactions of thousands of couples and identified the characteristics of those relationships likely to survive versus those that won't.

His research papers show his predictions are correct over 91 percent of the time.

First, you have to deal with conflict. If you criticize, act defensively, absent yourself (emotionally), or show contempt for your partner, your relationship is doomed. On the plus side, you can get away with anything if you say it in a warm, positive way. Perhaps your partner comes home, slumps in front of the television, and barely acknowledges you or the children. Now, you could say, "You selfish pig, you always sit in front of the television, you don't even say hello to me or the kids, you're a useless dad." This is what Gottman calls a "harsh start up." Compare a "soft start up": "It's lovely to see you, and it would really help me if you could play with the children while I finish up here." Now guess which one works better. Gottman advises a ratio of five positive comments to one negative comment when speaking to your partner, which could be challenging. Using humor, which is also effective in lightening up relationships and defusing conflict, may be more achievable.

So what about boredom? You need to do new and, I'm sorry to say, exciting things together. You must set aside time to go out, as a couple, on your own (not with more interesting couples). A study in the 1980s of eighty-seven married couples who had been together for fifteen years found they were good friends, enjoyed each other's company, and depended on each other. Researchers were struck by how affectionate the couples were to each other. And affection doesn't have to be a euphemism for "no sex." A recent study in the *British Medical Journal* of 1,506 adults all of whom were aged seventy found that the percentage of people saying their sex lives were good had increased between 1971 and 2001. The percentage of sexually happy men in this study rose from 40 to 57 percent and that of women from 35 to 52 percent.

Most long-term relationships seem to be happy. A study of 351 long-term couples in 1986 by researchers from the Southern Illinois University at Edwardsville found that 300 were happy. One husband told the researchers, "Commitment means a willingness to be unhappy for a while. You're not going to be happy with each other all the time."

Notes

1. Mr. or Ms. Right

Pickup Lines: Christopher Bale, Rory Morrison, and Peter G. Caryl, "Chat-up Lines as Male Sexual Displays," *Personality and Individual Differences* 40 (2006), 655–64.

Online Mating: Nicole Ellison, Rebecca Heino, and Jennifer Gibbs, "Managing Impressions Online: Self-presentation Processes in the Online Dating Environment," *Journal of Computer-Mediated Communication* 11, no. 2 (2006), 415–41. Jennifer Yurichisin, Kittichai Watchravespringkan, and Deborah Brown McRae, "An Exploration of Identity Recreation in the Context of Internet Dating," *Social Behavior and Personality* 33, no. 8 (2005), 735–50. University of Bath, press release, http://www.bathac.uk/pr/releases/Internet-dating.htm. Pew Internet and American Life Project. Online Dating: http://www.pewInternet.org/pdfs/PIP_Online_Dating.pdf.

Speedy Dating: Robert Kurzban and Jason Weeden, "HurryDate: Mate Preferences in Action," *Evolution and Human Behavior* 26 (2005), 227–44. U.S. Census Bureau, "College Degree Nearly Doubles Annual Earnings, Census Bureau Reports," press release, March 28, 2005, http://www.census.gov/Press-Release/www/releases/

archives/education/004214.html. Eli J. Finkle, Paul W. Eastwick, and J. Matthews, "Speed-dating as an Invaluable Tool for Studying Romantic Attraction: A Methodological Primer," *Personal Relationships* 14, no. 1 (2007), 149–66. Michele Belot and Marco Francesconi, "Can Anyone Be 'The' One? Evidence on Mate Selection from Speed Dating," University of Essex Discussion Paper (2006).

Romantic Timing: ComScore, Inc., "Just in Time for Valentine's Day, comScore Networks Reveals Top Dating Sites in the U.K., France and the U.S.," press release, February 12, 2007, http://www.comscore.com/press/release.asp?press=1204. Scripps Howard News Service, "Spring's Not the Favorite Season Nor a Time for Love," newspolls.org (2003).

In the Stars?: Pew Research Center for the People and the Press, "Many Americans Uneasy with Mix of Religion and Politics," August 24, 2006, http://people-press.org/report/?pageid=1084. David Voas, "Ten Million Marriages: A Test of Astrological 'Love Signs,'" University of Manchester (2007).

Birth Order: Ray Blanchard and Richard A. Lippa, "Birth Order, Sibling Sex Ratio, Handedness, and Sexual Orientation of Male and Female Participants in a BBC Internet Research Project," *Archives of Sexual Behavior* 36, no. 2 (2007), 163–76. Richard L. Michalski and Todd K. Shackleford, "Birth Order and Sexual Strategy," *Personality and Individual Differences* 33, no. 4 (2002), 661–67.

Wanted: Handsome Men: Satoshi Kanazawa, "Beautiful Parents Have More Daughters: A Further Implication of the Generalized Trivers-Willard Hypothesis," *Journal of Theoretical Biology* 244 (2007), 133–40.

Reeling from Rejection: Geraldine Downey, Antonio L. Freitas, Benjamin Michaelis, and Hala Khouri, "The Self-fulfilling Prophecy in Close Relationships: Rejection Sensitivity and Rejection by Romantic Partners," *Journal of Personality and Social Psychology* 75, no. 2 (1998), 545–60. A. Bifulco, P. M. Moran, C. Ball, and O. Bernazzani, "Adult Attachment Style. 1: Its Relationship to Clinical Depression," *Social Psychiatry and Psychiatric Epidemiology* 37, no. 2 (2002), 50–59. Geraldine Downey and Scott I. Feldman, "Implications of Rejection Sensitivity for Intimate Relationships," *Journal of Personality and Social Psychology* 70, no. 6 (1996), 1327–43.

Nice Guy But . . . : Geoffrey C. Urbaniak, "Physical Attractiveness and the 'Nice Guy Paradox': Do Nice Guys Really Finish Last?" *Sex Roles* 49

(2003), 413–26. Anita K. McDaniel, "Young Women's Dating Behavior: Why / Why Not Date a Nice Guy?" *Sex Roles* 53 (2005), 347–59.

Blonde or Brunette?: Peter Ayton, "How Do Men Feel about Women's Hair Colour?: A Survey of Male Attitudes and Reactions to Women's Hair," City University, London, (unpublished). Viren Swami, Adrian Furnham, and Kiran Joshi, "The Influence of Skin Tone, Hair Length, and Hair Colour on Ratings of Women's Physical Attractiveness, Health and Fertility," *Scandinavian Journal of Psychology* 49, no. 5 (2008), 429–37. Peter Frost, "European Hair and Eye Color. A Case of Frequency-dependent Sexual Selection?" *Evolution and Human Behavior* 27, no. 2 (2006), 85–103.

Dim View: C. J. Hammond, Toby Andrew, Ying Tat Mak, and Tim D. Spector, "A Susceptibility Locus for Myopia in the Normal Population Is Linked to the PAX6 Gene Region on Chromosome 11: A Genomewide Scan of Dizygotic Twins," *American Journal of Human Genetics* 75, no. 2 (2004), 294–304. C. J. Hammond, H. Snieder, Clare E. Gilbert, and Tim D. Spector, "Genes and Environment in Refractive Error: The Twin Eye Study," *Investigative Ophthalmology and Visual Science* 42, no. 6 (2001), 1232–36.

Big Egos: Joshua D. Foster and W. Keith Campbell, "Narcissism and Resistance to Doubts about Romantic Partners," *Journal of Research in Personality* 39, no. 5 (2005), 550–57. W. Keith Campbell and Craig A. Foster, "Narcissism and Commitment in Romantic Relationships: An Investment Model Analysis," *Personality and Social Psychology Bulletin* 28, no. 4 (2002), 484–95. Scott M. Stanley and Howard J. Markman, "Assessing Commitment in Personal Relationships," *Journal of Marriage and Family* 54 (1992), 595–608.

Freudian Blip: Christine B. Whelan, *Why Smart Men Marry Smart Women* (New York: Simon and Schuster, 2006). T. Bereczkei, Gabor Hegedus, and Gabor Hajnal, "Facialmetric Similarities Mediate Mate Choice: Sexual Imprinting on Opposite-sex Parents," *Proceedings of the Royal Society B* (2008). T. Bereczkei, P. Gyuris, P. Koves, and L. Bernath, "Homogamy, Genetic Similarity, and Imprinting: Parental Influence on Mate Choice Preferences," *Personality and Individual Differences* 33, no. 5 (2002), 677–90.

2. Opportunity Knocks

Poached Partners: David P. Schmitt and Todd K. Shackleford, "Nifty Ways to Leave Your Lover: The Tactics People Use to Entice and Disguise the Process of Human Mate Poaching," *Personality and Social Psychology Bulletin* 29, no. 8 (2003), 1018–35. David P. Schmitt and 121 members of the International Sexuality Description Project, "Patterns and Universals of Mate Poaching Across 53 Nations: The Effects of Sex, Culture, and Personality on Romantically Attracting Another Person's Partner," *Journal of Personality and Social Psychology* 86, no. 4 (2004), 560–84.

Office Romance: Lisa A. Mainiero, *Office Romance: Love, Power and Sex in the Workplace* (New York: Rawson Associates, 1989). Mary Loftus, "Frisky Business," *Psychology Today*, March/April 1995. "Office Romance," in *Encyclopedia of Small Businesses*, Endnotes.com, http://www.enotes.com/small-business-encyclopedia/office-romance.

One Night Only: Laura Bettor, Susan S. Hendrick, and Clyde Hendrick, "Gender and Sexual Standards in Dating Relationships," *Personal Relationships* 2, no. 4 (1995), 359–69. Edward S. Herold, Eleanor Maticka-Tyndale, and Dawn Mewhinney, "Predicting Intentions to Engage in Casual Sex," *Journal of Social and Personal Relationships* 15, no. 4 (1998), 502–16. Neal J. Rose, Ginger L. Pennington, Jill Coleman, Maria Janicki, Norman P. Li, and Douglas T. Kennick, "Sex Differences in Regret: All for Love or Some for Lust?" *Personality and Social Psychology Bulletin* 2, no. 6 (2006), 770–80. Sharon Hinchliff, "Women and One-night Stands," presented at the British Psychological Society's Annual Conference, March 2006.

Tall Story: D. Nettle, "Women's Height, Reproductive Success and the Evolution of Sexual Dimorphism in Modern Humans," *Proceedings of the Royal Society of London* (2002). James A. Shepperd and Alan J. Strathman, "Attractiveness and Height: The Role of Stature in Dating Preference, Frequency of Dating, and Perceptions of Attractiveness," *Personality and Social Psychology Bulletin* 15, no. 4 (1989), 617–27.

Dumb Choice: Michelle D. Taylor, Carole L. Hart, et al., "Childhood IQ and Marriage in Mid-life: The Scottish Mental Health Survey 1932 and the Midspan Studies," *Personality and Individual Differences* 38, no. 7 (2005), 1621–30. Bertjan Doosje, "Partner Preference as a Function of Gender, Age, Political Orientation, and Level of Education," *Sex Roles* 40, no. 1–2 (1999), 45–60. Megan M. Sweeny, "Two Decades of Family Change: The Shifting Economic Foundations of Marriage," *American Sociological Review* 67 (2002), 132–47. Heather Boushey's work is referenced at http://www.prospect.org/cs/articles?article=creating_a_lie.

First Mover: Jacquie D. Vorauer and Rebecca K. Ratner, "Who's Going to Make the First Move? Pluralistic Ignorance as an Impediment to Relationship Formation," *Journal of Social and Personal Relationships* 13, no. 4 (1996), 483–506.

Wish You Were Here: Michelle Thomas, "'What Happens in Tenerife Stays in Tenerife': Understanding Women's Sexual Behavior on Holiday," *Culture, Health and Sexuality* 7, no. 6 (2005), 571–84. J. Richard Eiser and Nicholas Ford, "Sexual Relationships on Holiday: A Case of Situational Disinhibition?" *Journal of Social and Personal Relationships* 12, no. 3 (1995), 323–39. "The Summer Holiday," MORI: http://extranet.ipsos-mori.com/polls/1998/nfm3.shtml.

Ex or Hex?: April L. Bleske and Todd K. Shackleford, "Poaching, Promiscuity, and Deceit: Combating Mating Rivalry in Same-sex Friendships," *Personal Relationships* 8, no. 4 (2005), 407–24. David P. Schmitt and Todd K. Shackleford, "Nifty Ways to Leave Your Lover: The Tactics People Use to Entice and Disguise the Process of Human Mate Poaching," *Personality and Social Psychology Bulletin* 29, no. 8 (2003), 1018–35. David P. Schmitt and 121 members of the International Sexuality Description Project, "Patterns and Universals of Mate Poaching Across 53 Nations: The Effects of Sex, Culture, and Personality on Romantically Attracting Another Person's Partner," *Journal of Personality and Social Psychology* 86, no. 4 (2004), 560–84.

Unsettling Thoughts: Pamela C. Regan, "What if You Can't Get What You Want? Willingness to Compromise Ideal Mate Selection Standards as a Function of Sex, Mate Value, and Relationship Context," *Personality and Social Psychology Bulletin* 24, no. 12 (1998), 1294–303. "An Iconic Report 20 Years Later: Many of Those Women Married After All," http://www.wsj.com/public/article/SB114852493706762691.html. Evelyn L. Lehrer, "Age at Marriage and Marital Instability: Revisiting the Becker-Landes-Michael Hypothesis," *Journal of Population Economics* 21, no. 2 (2008), 463–84. C. Ayles, *Biographical Determinants of Marital Quality* (London: One Plus One, 2004). Robyn Parker, *Relationships Indicators Survey, 2006* (Melbourne: Australian Institute of Family Studies, 2006). Pew Research Center, *As Marriage and Parenthood Drift Apart, Public Is Concerned about Social Impact* (Washington, D.C.: Pew Research Center, 2007).

Rebound to Fail?: Nicholas H. Wolfinger, "Does the Rebound Effect Exist? Time to Remarriage and Subsequent Union Stability," *Journal of Divorce and Remarriage* 46 (2007), 9–20. J. S. Wallerstein and J. B. Kelly, *Surviving the Breakup: How Children and Parents Cope with Divorce* (New York: Basic Books, 1980). John Ermisch, "Trying Again: Repartnering after Dissolution of a Union," ISER Working Papers no. 2002–19.

3. After the First Few Dates

Can't Hurry Love: Robert Milardo, University of Maine, personal communication. C. Hendricks, *Romantic Love* (Beverly Hills, Calif.: Sage, 1992).

Friendly Fire: Susan Sprecher and Diane Felmlee,"The Influence of Parents and Friends on the Quality and Stability of Romantic Relationships: A Three-wave Longitudinal Investigation," *Journal of Marriage and Family* 54 (1992), 888–900. Justin J. Lehmiller and Christopher R. Agnew, "Marginalized Relationships: The Impact of Social Disapproval on Romantic Relationship Commitment," *Personality and Psychology Bulletin* 32 (2006), 40–51.

Round the Bend: *Sex Differences in Driving and Insurance Risk*, Social Issues Research Center, August 2004. "Women Drivers 'Better' Claim Proved," BBC News, http://www.news.bbc.co.uk/1/hi/wales/1590309.stm. "Men Driving Women Around the Bend on British Roads," ICM survey, April 13, 2007, icmresearch.co.uk. Lawrence A. Kurdek, "Predicting Change in Marital Satisfaction from Husbands' and Wives' Conflict Resolution Styles," *Journal of Marriage and Family* 57, no. 1 (1995), 153–64. Dow Chang, "Comparison of Crash Fatalities by Sex and Age Group," National Highway Traffic Safety Administration, July 2008, http://www-nrd.nhtsa.dot.gov/Pubs/810853.pdf. Jacqueline Bergdahl and Michael

R. Norris, "Sex Differences in Single Vehicle Fatal Crashes: A Research Note," *Social Science* 39, no. 2 (2002), 287–93. Guohua Li, Susan P. Baker, Jean A. Langlois, and Gabor D. Kelen, "Are Female Drivers Safer? An Application of the Decomposition Method," *Epidemiology* 9, no. 4 (1998), 379–84.

Split the Difference?: Hongyu Wang and Paul R. Amato, "Predictors of Divorce Adjustment: Stressors, Resources, and Definitions," *Journal of Marriage and Family* 62, no. 3 (2000), 655–68. John Haskey, "Divorce and Remarriage in England and Wales," *Population Trends* 95 (1999), 7–17. Nehami Baum, "The Male Way of Mourning Divorce: When, What and How," *Clinical Social Work Journal* 31, no. 1 (2003), 37–50.

Romeo and Juliet: Craig A. Foster and W. Keith Campbell, "The Adversity of Secret Relationships," *Personal Relationships* 12 (2005), 125–43. Leslie A. Baxter and Sally Widenmann, "Revealing and Not Revealing the Status of Romantic Relationships to Social Networks," *Journal of Social and Personal Relationships* 10 (1993), 321–36.

Poles Apart: Anna P. Puvolo and Lisa A. Fabin, "Two of a Kind: Perceptions of Own and Partner's Attachment Characteristics," *Personal Relationships* 6, no. 1 (1999), 57–79. Shanhong Luo and Eva C. Klohnen, "Assortative Mating and Marital Quality in Newlyweds: A Couple-centered Approach," *Journal of Personality and Social Psychology* 88, no. 2 (2005), 304–26. Joel A. Gold, Richard M. Ryckman, and Norman R. Mosley, "Romantic Mood Induction and Attraction to a Dissimilar Other: Is Love Blind?" *Personality and Social Psychology Bulletin* 10, no. 3 (1984), 358–68.

Controlling the Remote: Alexis J. Walker, "Couples Watching Television: Gender, Power and the Remote Control," *Journal of Marriage and Family* 58 (1996), 813–23. David Morley, *Family Television: Cultural Power and Domestic Leisure* (New York and London: Routledge, 1986).

Sex and Lies: Michele G. Alexander and Terri D. Fisher, "Truth and Consequences: Using the Bogus Pipeline to Examine Sex Differences in Self-reported Sexuality," *Journal of Sex Research* 40 (2003), 27. Norman R. Brown and Robert C. Sinclair, "Estimating Number of Lifetime Sexual Partners: Men and Women Do It Differently," *Journal of Sex Research* 36 (1999), 292–97. Devon D. Brewer, John J. Potterat, Sharon B. Garrett, Stephen Q. Muth, John

M. Roberts Jr., Danuta Kasprzyk, Daniel E. Montano, and William W. Darrow, "Prostitution and the Sex Discrepancy in Reported Number of Sexual Partners," *Proceedings of the National Academy of Sciences* 97, no. 22 (2000), 12385–88. Centers for Disease Control and Prevention, "Advance Data from Vital and Health Statistics," no. 362, September 15, 2005, http://www.cdc.gov/nchs/data/ad/ad362.pdf. Lindsay A. Wittrock, "The Gender Discrepancy in Reported Number of Sexual Partners: Effects of Anonymity," *Journal of Undergraduate Research* 7 (2004), http://www.uwlax.edu/URC/JUR-online/PDF/2004/wittrock.pdf. Susan Sprecher, Pamela C. Regan, Kathleen McKinney, Kallye Maxwell, and Robert Wazienski, "Preferred Level of Sexual Experience in a Date or Mate: The Merger of Two Methodologies," *Journal of Sex Research* 34, no. 4 (1997), 327–37.

Kiss Off: Andrea Demirjian, *Kissing* (London: Penguin, 2006). Susan M. Hughes, Marissa A. Harrison, and Gordon G. Gallup, Jr., "Sex Differences in Romantic Kissing Among College Students: An Evolutionary Perspective," *Evolutionary Psychology* 5, no. 3 (2007), 612–31.

I Was Only Saying . . . : Frank F. Fisham, Julie Hall, and Steven R. H. Beach, "Forgiveness in Marriage: Current Status and Future Directions," *Family Relations* 55, no. 4 (2006), 415–27. Linda J. Roberts, "Fire and Ice in Marital Communications: Hostile and Distancing Behaviors as Predictors of Marital Distress," *Journal of Marriage and Family* 62 (2000), 693–707. "Decade Review: Observing Marital Interaction," *Journal of Marriage and Family* 62 (2000), 927–94.

4. What Happens Next?

Going the Distance: Long Distance Relationships, http://www.longdistancerelationships.net/about_the_center.htm. Mary Holmes, "Living Love at Long-Distance: Intimacy in Couples Who Live Apart," *Economic and Social Research Council*, RES-000-22-0351 (2006).

Homeward Bound: Laura Stafford and Andy J. Merolla, "Idealization, Reunions, and Stability in Long-distance Dating Relationships," *Journal of Social and Personal Relationships* 24, no. 1 (2007), 37–54. Laura Stafford, Andy J. Merolla, and Janessa D. Castle, "When Long-distance Dating Partners Become Geographically Close," *Journal of Social and Personal Relationships* 23, no. 6 (2006), 901–19.

Faith in Our Relationship: Inter-ethnic marriage, national statistics, http://www.statistics.gov.uk, 2006. F. L. Jones, "Convergence and Divergence in Ethnic Divorce Patterns: A Research Note," *Journal of Marriage and Family* 58 (1996), 213–18.

Toy Boy or Not Toy Boy?: Ní Bhrolcháin Máire, "The Age Difference at Marriage in England and Wales: A Century of Patterns and Trends," *Population Trends* 120 (2005), 7–14. "Women Marrying Younger Men, England and Wales," One Plus One, http://www.oneplusone.org.uk/ICOR/StatisticsDetails.php?Ref=44. Jacqueline E. Darroch, David J. Landry, and Selene Oslak, "Age Differences Between Sexual Partners in the United States," *Family Planning Perspectives* 31, no. 4 (1999), 160–67. "Cougars and Their Cubs," AARP.org, http://www.aarp.org/family/love/articles/cougars_and_their.html.

My Valentine: "Valentine's Day Romance," survey by Blue Nile, February 2006, http://www.bluenile.com. Harris Interactive, "Lifestyles Condoms Valentine's Day Survey," February 2006. "Ideal Couples and Romance," *Psychology Today*, http://www.psychologytoday.com/articles/index.php?/term=pto-19950301–000027&pr.

Stop or Shop: Sharon Sassler, "The Process of Entering into Cohabiting Unions," *Journal of Marriage and Family* 66, no. 2 (May 2004), 491–506.

He's Not the One: The National Marriage Project, "The State of Our Unions 2001," Rutgers University, New Brunswick, N.J. Ann P. Ruvolo and Catherine M. Ruvolo, "Creating Mr. Right and Ms. Right: Interpersonal Ideals and Personal Change in Newlyweds," *Personal Relationships* 7, no. 4 (2005), 341–62. Neil Clark Warren, *Falling in Love for All the Right Reasons* (New York: Hachette, 2005).

Getting to "Yes": Catherine A. Surra and Debra K. Hughes, "Commitment Processes in Accounts of the Development of Premarital Relationships," *Journal of Marriage and Family* 59, no. 1 (1997), 5–21. James H. Tolhuizen, "Communication Strategies for Intensifying Dating Relationships: Identification, Use and Structure," *Journal of Social and Personal Relationships* 6 (1989), 4113. National Healthy Marriage Resource Center, "Frequently Asked Questions about Commitment," http://www.healthymarriageinfo.org/research.

Marry without Haste: Scott M. Stanley, Galena Kline Rhoades, and Howard J. Markman, "Sliding Versus Deciding: Inertia and the

Premarital Cohabiting Effect," *Family Relations* 55 (October 2006), 499–509. One Plus One, "Married or Not in Britain Today," http://www.oneplusone.org.uk. *Focus on Families* (New York: Palgrave Macmillan, 2007), http://www.statistics.gov.uk/focuson/families. David de Vaus, Lixia Qu, and Ruth Weston, "Premarital Cohabitation and Subsequent Marital Stability," *Family Matters* 65 (2003), 34–39. Anne-Marie Ambert, *Cohabitation and Marriage: How Are They Related?* (Ottawa, Ont.: Vanier Institute of the Family, 2006). Claire M. Kamp Dush, Catherine L. Cohan, and Paul R. Amato, "The Relationship Between Cohabitation and Marital Quality and Stability: Change Across Cohorts?" *Journal of Marriage and Family* 65, no. 3 (2003), 539–50.

Love Match Has Catch: Amitrajeet A. Batabyal, *Stochastic Models of Decision Making in Arranged Marriages* (Lanham, Md.: University Press of America, 2006). Xu Xiaohe and Martin King Whyte, "Love Matches and Arranged Marriages: A Chinese Replication," *Journal of Marriage and Family* 52, no. 3 (1990), 709–22. "Divorce Rate in India," Divorcerate.org, http://www.divorcerate.org/divorce-rate-in-india.html. "40% Divorce Rate in Mumbai, India," South Asian Connection, http://www.southasianconnection.com/blogs/607/40-Divorce-Rate-In-Mumbai-India.

What's in a Name?: Marie-France Valetas, "The Surname of Married Women in the European Union," *Population and Societies* 367 (2001). Claudia Goldin and Maria Shim, "Making a Name: Women's Surnames at Marriage and Beyond," *Journal of Economic Perspectives* 18, no. 2 (2004), 143–60.

Looking Good?: Verlin B. Hinsz, "Facial Resemblance in Engaged and Married Couples," *Journal of Social and Personal Relationships* 6, no. 2 (1989), 223–29. Gregory L. White, "Physical Attractiveness and Courtship Progress," *Journal of Personality and Social Psychology* 39, no. 4 (1980), 660–68. James K. McNulty, Lisa A. Neff, and Benjamin R. Karney, "Beyond Initial Attraction: Physical Attractiveness in Newlywed Marriage," *Journal of Family Psychology* 22, no. 1 (2008), 133–43.

5. Jealousy and Affairs

Men in Uniform: Nicole A. Roberts and Robert W. Levenson, "The Remains of the Workday: Impact of Job Stress and Exhaustion on

Marital Interaction in Police Couples," *Journal of Marriage and Family* 63, no. 4 (2001), 10052–67. Corneil Askew, "Managing Stress and Traumatic Stress Incidents," an applied paper submitted to the Department of Interdisciplinary Technology, Eastern Michigan University (2004). Bruce L. Rollman, Lucy A. Mead, Nae-Yuh Wang, and Michael J. Klag, "Medical Specialty and the Incidence of Divorce," *New England Journal of Medicine* 336 (1997), 800–3.

New Company: Michael Svarer, "Working Late: Do Workplace Sex Ratios Affect Partnership Formation and Dissolution?" *Journal of Human Resources* 42, no. 3 (2007), 582–95. Derek Kemp, *Work–Love Balance* (Amersham, England: Human and Legal Resources, 2004).

Is She Faithful?: Anna R. McAlister, Nancy Pachana, and Chris J. Jackson, "Predictors of Young Dating Adults' Inclination to Engage in Extradyadic Sexual Activities: A Multi-perspective Study," *British Journal of Psychology* 96, no. 3 (2005), 331–50. "Infidelity," Menstuff, http://www.menstuff.org/issues/byissue/infidelity.html (2008). "Your Unadulterated Thoughts on Adultery," MSNBC.com, http://www.msnbc.msn.com/id/18055526 (2007). M. Fine and J. Harvey, eds., *The Handbook of Divorce and Romantic Dissolution* (New York: Psychology Press, 2005).

Me or the Missus?: Jan Halper, *Quiet Desperation: The Truth About Successful Men* (New York: Warner Books, 1988). Lana Staheli, *Affair-Proof Your Marriage* (New York: Harper Perennial, 1998). Frank Pittman, *Private Lies: Infidelity and the Betrayal of Intimacy* (New York: Norton, 1989). Ruth Houston, *Is He Cheating On You?: 829 Telltale Signs* (Elmhurst, N.Y.: Lifestyle, 2002).

Too Many Cooks: Elaine Cook, "Commitment in Polyamorous Relationships," http://www.aphroweb.com. Dale Wachowiak and Hannelore Bragg, "Open Marriages and Marital Adjustment," *Journal of Marriage and Family* 42, no. 1 (1980), 57–62. Geri D. Weitzman, "What Psychology Professionals Should Know About Polyamory," http://www.polyamory.org/-joe/polypaper.htm.

Green-eyed Monster: Leanne K. Knobloch, Denise Haunani Solomon, and Michael G. Cruz, "The Role of Relationship Development and Attachment in the Experience of Romantic Jealousy," *Personal Relationships* 8, no. 2 (2001), 205–34. Stephen M. Yoshimura, "Emotional and Behavioral Responses to Romantic Jealousy Expressions," *Communication Reports* 17, no. 2 (2004), 85–101. Gary L.

Hansen, "Reactions to Hypothetical Jealousy-producing Events," *Family Relations* 31, no. 4 (1982), 510–18.

Flirt Alert: Amy A. Fleischmann, Brian H. Spitzberg, Peter A. Anderson, and Scott C. Roesch, "Tickling the Monster: Jealousy Induction in Relationships," *Journal of Social and Personal Relationships* 22, no. 1 (2005), 49–73. Monica T. Whitty, "Cyber-flirting: An Examination of Men's and Women's Flirting Behavior Both Offline and on the Internet," *Behavior Change* 21, no. 2 (2004), 115–27. Kate Fox, *SIRC Guide to Flirting*, Social Issues Research Center, http://www.sirc.org/publik/flirt.html.

Truth or Dare?: Kinsey Institute, "Frequently Asked Questions," http://www.kinseyinstitute.org/resources/FAQ/html. Walid A. Afifi, Wendy L. Falato, and Judith L. Weiner, "Identity Concerns Following a Severe Relational Transgression: The Role of Discovery Method for the Relational Outcomes of Infidelity," *Journal of Social and Personal Relationships* 18, no. 2 (2001), 291–308. M. A. Tafoya and B. H. Spitzberg, "Communicative Infidelity," in *The Dark Side of Interpersonal Communication* (2nd ed.), ed. B. H. Spitzberg and W. R. Cupach (Mahwah, N.J.: Lawrence Erlbaum, 2007), 199–242.

Just Good Friends: Vickie Harvey, " 'We're Just Friends': Myth Construction as a Communication Strategy in Communicating Cross-sex Friendships," *Qualitative Report* 8, no. 2 (2003), 314–32. April L. Bleske and David M. Buss, "Can Men and Women Just be Friends?" *Personal Relationships* 7, no. 2 (2000), 131–51.

6. Break-ups or Make-ups?

Revenge Is Sour: Stephen Yoshimura, "Goals and Emotional Outcomes of Revenge Activities in Interpersonal Relationships," *Journal of Social and Personal Relationships* 24, no. 1 (2007), 8.

Post-Traumatic Love Disorder: Ellen J. Pettit and Bernard L. Bloom, "Whose Decision Was It? The Effects of Initiator Status on Adjustment to Marital Disruption," *Journal of Marriage and Family* 46, no. 3 (1984), 587–95. Y. Arieh and J. Shalev, "What Is Posttraumatic Stress Disorder?" *Clinical Psychiatry* 62, suppl. 17 (2001), 4–10. Zheng Wu and Randy Hart, "The Effects of Marital and Nonmarital Union Transition on Health," *Journal of Marriage and Family* 64, no. 2 (2002), 420–33.

Tears before Bedtime: A. Najib, J. P. Lorberbaum, S. Kose, D. E. Binning, and M. S. George, "Regional Brain Activity in Women Grieving a Romantic Relationship Breakup," *American Journal of Psychiatry* 161 (2004), 2245–56.

Unfair Affair: Roy F. Baumeister, Sara R. Wotman, and Arlene M. Stillwell, "Unrequited Love: On Heartbreak, Anger, Guilt, Scriptlessness, and Humiliation," *Journal of Personality and Social Psychology* 64, no. 3 (1993), 377–94. Arthur Aron, Elaine N. Aron, and Josephine Allen, "Motivations for Unreciprocated Love," *Personality and Social Psychology Bulletin* 24, no. 8 (1998), 787–96.

Cuddling Deficiency: Daniel J. Weigel and Deborah S. Ballard-Reisch, "Investigating the Behavioral Indicators of Relational Commitment," *Journal of Social and Personal Relationships* 19, no. 3 (2002), 403–23. Laura K. Guerrero and Peter A. Andersen, "The Waxing and Waning of Relational Intimacy: Touch as a Function of Relational Stage, Gender and Touch Avoidance," *Journal of Social and Personal Relationships* 8, no. 2 (1991), 147–65.

Alpha Male Alert: Kim Bartholomew, "Avoidance of Intimacy: An Attachment Perspective," *Journal of Social and Personal Relationships* 7, no. 2 (1990), 147–75. Linda K. Acitelli, David A. Kenny, and Debra Weiner, "The Importance of Similarity and Understanding of Partners' Marital Ideals to Relationship Satisfaction," *Personal Relationships* 8, no. 2 (2001), 167–85. Peter M. Buston and Stephen T. Emlen, "Cognitive Processes Underlying Human Mate Choice: The Relationship Between Self-perception and Mate Preference in Western Society," *Proceedings of the National Academy of Sciences* 100, no. 15 (2003), 8805–10.

Gone for Good?: E. J. Pettit and B. L. Bloom, "Whose Decision Was It?: The Effect of Initiator Status on Adjustment to Marital Disruption," *Journal of Marriage and Family* 46, no. 3 (1994), 587–96. Georgina Binstock and Arland Thornton, "Separations, Reconciliations and Living Apart in Cohabiting and Marital Union," *Journal of Marriage and Family* 65, no. 2 (2003), 432–43. Jeffry A. Simpson, "The Dissolution of Romantic Relationships: Factors Involved in Relationship Stability and Emotional Distress," *Journal of Personality and Social Psychology* 53, no. 4 (1987), 683–92.

Gullible or Gutted?: Straight Spouse, http://www.straightspouse.org. Dorothea Hays and Aurele Samuels, "Heterosexual Women's Perceptions of Their Marriages to Bisexual or Homosexual Men,"

Journal of Homosexuality 18 (1989), 81–100. Anne Johnson, Catherine H. Mercer, Bob Erens, Andrew J. Copas, Sally McManus, Kaye Wellings, et al., "Sexual Behavior in Britain: Partnerships, Practices, and HIV Risk Behaviors," *Lancet* 358 (2001), 1835–42. Michael W. Ross, "Married Homosexual Men: Prevalence and Background," *Marriage and Family Review* 14 (1989), 35. Amity Pierce Buxton, "Paths and Pitfalls: How Heterosexual Spouses Cope When their Husbands or Wives Come Out," in *Relationship Therapy with Same-sex Couples*, ed. J. J. Bigner and J. L. Wetchler (Binghamton, N.Y.: Haworth Press, 2004). Amity Pierce Buxton,"When a Spouse Comes Out as Gay, Lesbian or Bisexual," in *An Introduction to GLBT Family Studies*, ed. J. J. Bigner (Binghamton, N.Y.: Haworth Press, 2006), 67–88. H. Laurence Ross, "Modes of Adjustments of Married Homosexuals," *Social Problems* 18, no. 3 (1971), 385–93.

In the Genes?: Paul R. Amato and Jacob Cheadle, "The Long Reach of Divorce: Divorce and Child Well-being Across Three Generations," *Journal of Family and Marriage* 67, no. 1 (2005), 191–206. Valerie King, "Parental Divorce and Interpersonal Trust in Adult Offspring," *Journal of Marriage and Family* 64, no. 3 (2002), 642–56. Paul R. Amato and Danelle D. DeBoer, "The Transmission of Marital Instability Across Generations: Relationship Skills or Commitment to Marriage?" *Journal of Marriage and Family* 63, no. 4 (2001), 1038–51. Susan E. Jacques and Catherine A. Surra, "Parental Divorce and Premarital Couples: Commitment and Other Relationship Characteristics," *Journal of Marriage and Family* 63, no. 4 (2001), 627–39.

Third Time Lucky?: Larry Bumpass, James Sweet, and Teresa Castro Martin, "Changing Patterns of Remarriage," *Journal of Marriage and Family* 52, no. 3 (1990), 747–56. One Plus One, Frequently Asked Questions, http://www.oneplusone.org.uk/faqs.asp. Norval D. Glenn and Charles N. Weaver, "The Marital Happiness of Remarried Divorced Persons," *Journal of Marriage and Family* 39, no. 2 (1977), 331–37. Marilyn Coleman, Lawrence Ganong, and Mark Fine,"Reinvestigating Remarriage: Another Decade of Progress," *Journal of Marriage and Family* 62, no. 4 (2000), 1288–307.

7. Sex Lives

Tri-weekly: F. Scott Christopher and Susan Sprecher, "Sexuality in Marriage, Dating and Other Relationships: A Decade Review," *Journal of Marriage and Family* 62, no. 4 (2000), 999–1017. E. Sandra Byers and Stephanie Demmons, "Sexual Satisfaction and Sexual Self-disclosure within Dating Relationships," *Journal of Sex Research* 36, no. 2 (1999), 180–89. Cathy Stein Greenblat, "The Saliency of Sexuality in the Early Years of Marriage," *Journal of Marriage and Family* 45, no. 2 (1993), 289–99.

Try Weekly: Edward O. Laumann, Anthony Palk, and Raymond C. Rosen, "Sexual Dysfunction in the United States," *Journal of the American Medical Association* 282, 13 (1999), 537–44. Graham Hart and Kaye Wellings, "Sexual Behavior and Its Medicalisation: In Sickness and in Health," *British Medical Journal* 324 (2002), 896–900.

Try Weakly: Irwin Nazareth, Petra Boynton, and Michael King, "Problems with Sexual Function in People Attending London General Practitioners: Cross-sectional Study," *British Medical Journal* 327 (2003), 425–31. Stephanie Davies, Jennifer Katz, and Joan L. Jackson, "Sexual Desire Discrepancies: Effects on Sexual and Relationship Satisfaction in Heterosexual Dating Couples," *Archives of Sexual Behavior* 28, no. 6 (1999), 553–68.

Dream On: Eileen L. Zurbriggen and Megan R. Yost, "Power, Desire, and Pleasure in Sexual Fantasies," *Journal of Sex Research* 41 (2004), 288–99. Thomas V. Hicks and Harold Leitenberg, "Sexual Fantasies about One's Partner versus Someone Else: Gender Differences in Incidence and Frequency," *Journal of Sex Research* 38 (2001), 43–50. Marta Meana and Sarah E. Nunnink, "Gender Differences in the Content of Cognitive Distraction During Sex," *Journal of Sex Research* 43 (2006), 59–67.

Addicted to Love: John Bancroft and Zoran Vukadinovic, "Sexual Addiction, Sexual Compulsivity, Sexual Impulsivity, or What?: Toward a Theoretical Model," *Journal of Sex Research* 41, no. 3 (2004), 225–34. Jennifer P. Schneider, "How to Recognize the Signs of Sexual Addiction," *Postgraduate Medicine* 90, no. 6 (1991), 177–82.

Sex Toys: Lesley A. Yee and Kendra J. Sundquist, "Older Women's Sexuality," *Medical Journal of Australia* 178, no. 12 (2003), 640–43. Phyllis K. Mansfield, Patricia B. Koch, and Ann M. Voda, "Qualities

Midlife Women Desire in Their Sexual Relationships and Their Changing Sexual Response," *Psychology of Women Quarterly* 22, no. 2 (2006), 285–303.

Just for the Celibate: Denise A. Donnelly and Elisabeth O. Burgess, "The Decision to Remain in an Involuntary Celibate Relationship," *Journal of Marriage and Family* 70, no. 2 (2008), 519–35.

It's Width Not Length: Willibrond Weijmar Schultz, Pek van Andel, Ida Sabelis, and Edyard Mooyaart, "Magnetic Resonance Imaging of Male and Female Genitals During Coitus and Female Sexual Arousal," *British Medical Journal* 319 (1999), 1596–99. H. Wessells, T. F. Lue, and J. W. McAnich, "Penile Length in the Flaccid and Erect States: Guidelines for Penile Augmentation," *Journal of Urology* 156, no. 3 (1996), 995–97. N. Mondaini, R. Ponchietti, P. Gontero, G. H. Muir, A. Natali, E. Caldarera, S. Biscioni, and M. Rizzo, "Penile Length Is Normal in Most Men Seeking Penile Lengthening Procedures," *International Journal of Impotence Research* 14, no. 4 (2002), 283–86.

Save Sex: Kaiser Family Foundation, "Sexual Health Statistics for Teenagers and Young Adults in the United States," September 2006, www.kff.org. Guttmacher Institute, "Facts on American Teens' Sexual and Reproductive Health," September 2006, http://www.guttmacher.org/pubs/fb_ATSRH.html. David Knox and Kenneth Wilson, "Dating Behaviors of University Students," *Family Relations* 30 (1981), 255–58.

Neurotic Erotic: Ana J. Bridges, Raymond M. Bergner, and Matthew Hesson-Mcinnis, "Romantic Partners' Use of Pornography: Its Significance for Women," *Journal of Sex and Marital Therapy* 29, no. 1 (2003), 1–14. Sarah O'Reilly, David Knox, and Marty E. Zusman, "College Student Attitudes Towards Pornography Use," *College Student Journal* 41, no. 2 (2007), 402–8.

Born to Use Porn?: Heather A. Rupp and Kim Wallen, "Sex Differences in Response to Visual Sexual Stimuli: A Review," *Archives of Sexual Behavior* 37, no. 2 (2008), 206–18. Gert Martin Hald, "Gender Differences in Pornography Consumption among Young Heterosexual Danish Adults," *Archives of Sexual Behavior* 35, no. 5 (2006), 577–85. Clarissa Smith, *One For the Girls!* (Bristol, England: Intellect Books, 2007).

8. Surviving Children

Bundle of Joy?: J. M. Twenge, W. K. Campbell, and C. A. Foster, "Parenthood and Marital Satisfaction: A Meta-analytic Review," *Journal of Marriage and Family* 65, no. 3 (2003), 574–83. Alyson Shapiro, John Gottman, et al., "The Baby and the Marriage: Identifying Factors that Buffer Against Decline in Marital Satisfaction After the First Baby Arrives," *Journal of Family Psychology* 14, no. 1 (2000), 59–70. Khi M. Nomaguchi and Melissa A. Milkie, "Costs and Rewards of Children: The Effects of Becoming a Parent on Adults' Lives," *Journal of Marriage and Family* 65, no. 2 (2003), 356–74. Jay Belsky and Michael Rovine, "Patterns of Marital Change Across the Transition to Parenthood: Pregnancy to Three Years Postpartum," *Journal of Marriage and Family* 52, no. 1 (1990), 5–19. Martha J. Cox, Blair Paley, Margaret Burchinal, and C. Chris Payne, "Marital Perceptions and Interactions Across the Transition to Parenthood," *Journal of Marriage and Family* 61, no. 3 (1999), 611–25. One Plus One, *The Transition to Parenthood—The Magic Moment*, http://www.theparentconnection.org.uk.

Changing Minds: Jacinta Bronte-Tinkew, Suzanne Ryan, Jennifer Carrano, and Kristin A. Moore, "Resident Father's Pregnancy Intentions, Prenatal Behaviors, and Links to Involvement with Infants," *Journal of Marriage and Family* 69, no. 4 (2007), 977–90. Kay Pasley, Ted G. Futris, and Martie L. Skinner, "Effects of Commitment and Psychological Centrality on Fathering," *Journal of Marriage and Family* 64, no. 1 (2002), 130–38. David J. Eggebeen and Chris Knoester, "Does Fatherhood Matter for Men?" *Journal of Marriage and Family* 63, no. 2 (2001), 381–93.

Impact of Infertility: Arthur L. Griel, "Infertility and Psychological Distress: A Critical Review of the Literature," paper presented to annual meeting of the Society for the Study of Social Problems, August 1993. Brennan D. Peterson, Christopher R. Newton, Karen H. Rosen, and Robert S. Schulman, "Coping Processes of Couples Experiencing Infertility," *Family Relations* 55 (2006), 227–39. Judith C. Daniluk, "Reconstructing Their Lives: A Longitudinal, Qualitative Analysis of the Transition to Biological Childlessness for Infertile Couples," *Journal of Counselling and Development* 79 (2001), 439–49. L. Repokari, R.-L. Punamaki, L. Unkila-Kallio, S. Vilska,

P. Poikkeus, J. Sinkkonen, F. Almqvist, A. Tiitinen, and M. Tulppala, "Infertility Treatment and Marital Relationships: A 1-year Prospective Study Among Successfully Treated ART Couples and Their Controls," *Human Reproduction* 22, no. 5 (2007), 1481–91.

Seasonal Birth Disorders: National Statistics Quarterly, Spring 2001, Stationery Office, London, 2001. E. Fuller Torrey, Judy Miller, Robert Rawlings, and Robert H. Yolken, "Seasonal Birth Patterns of Neurological Disorders," *Neuro-epidemiology* 19, no. 4 (2000), 177–85. A. Ivarsson, O. Hernell, L. Nystrom, and L. A. Pearson, "Children Born in the Summer Have Increased Risk for Celiac Disease," *Journal of Epidemiology and Community Health* 57, no. 1 (2003), 36–39. Emad Salib and Mario Cortina-Borja, "Effects of Month of Birth on the Risk of Suicide," *British Journal of Psychiatry* 188 (2006), 416–22. Robert Goodman, Julia Gledhill, and Tasmin Ford, "Child Psychiatric Disorder and Relative Age within School Year: Cross-sectional Survey of Large Population Sample," *British Medical Journal* 327 (2003), 472. Christen J. Willer, David A. Dyment, A. Dessa Sadovnick, Peter M. Rothwell, T. Jock Murray, and George C. Eberes, "Timing of Birth and Risk of Multiple Sclerosis: Population-based Study," *British Medical Journal* 330 (2005), 120. Henrik Toft Sorenson, Lars Pederson, Bente Norgard, Kirsten Fonager, and Kenneth J. Rothman, "Does Month of Birth Affect Risk of Crohn's Disease in Children and Adolescence?" *British Medical Journal* 323 (2001), 907.

Kids as Contraceptives: F. Scott Christopher and Susan Sprecher, "Sexuality in Marriage, Dating and Other Relationships: A Decade Review," *Journal of Marriage and Family* 62, no. 4 (2000), 999–1017. Janet Shibley Hyde, John D. DeLamamter, Ashley E. Pant, and Janis M. Byrd, "Sexuality During Pregnancy and the Year Postpartum," *Journal of Sex Research* 33, no. 2 (1996), 143–52. Jay Belsky and Michael Rovine, "Patterns of Marital Change Across the Transition to Parenthood: Pregnancy to Three Years Postpartum," *Journal of Marriage and Family* 52, no. 1 (1990), 5–19.

Step to Take: Susan D. Stewart, "How the Birth of a Child Affects Involvement with Stepchildren," *Journal of Marriage and Family* 67, no. 2 (2005), 461–73. A. Adeyemo and Grace Igaba Omongha, "Stepparents' Perception of the Factors Affecting the Quality of the Stepparent/Stepchild Relationship," *Journal of Human Ecology* 23, no. 2 (2008), 91–99. Joseph Rowntree Foundation, *Step-parenting in the*

1990s, ref. no. 658. Economic and Social Research Council (London), "Stepfamilies and Lone Parents: Changing Family Life in Britain," press release, June 30, 2007.

For the Kids: National Marriage Project, *The State of our Unions: The Social Health of Marriage in America, 2001* (Rutgers University, New Brunswick, N.J.) Ann-Marie Ambert, *Divorce: Facts, Causes, and Consequences* (Ottawa, Ont.: Vanier Institute of the Family, 2005). Daniel N. Hawkins and Alan Booth, "Unhappily Ever After: Effects of Long-term, Low-quality Marriages on Well-being," *Social Forces* 84, no. 1 (2005), 451–71. Frank F. Furstenberg and Kathleen E. Kiernan, "Delayed Parental Divorce: How Much Do Children Benefit?" *Journal of Marriage and Family* 63, no. 2 (2001), 446–57.

9. Testing Times

First Feelings: You can find Dr. Kalish at http://www.nancykalish.com. Nancy Kalish, "Rekindling Romance: Seniors who Find Lost Loves," http://www.lostlovers.com/reports.htm. Nancy Kalish, "2001, A Cyberspace Odyssey, Friends and Lovers: Connecting Past and Present Via the Internet," a paper presented to the 109th Annual Convention of the American Psychological Association, 2001. Nancy Kalish, "Adults Who Reunited with Their Adolescent Sweethearts: A Survey," a paper presented to the 108th Annual Convention of the American Psychological Association, 2000. M. Wegner-Daniel and B. Gold-Daniel, "Fanning Old Flames: Emotional and Cognitive Effects of Suppressing Thoughts of a Past Relationship," *Journal of Personality and Social Psychology* 68, no. 5 (1995), 782–92.

Fatal Attraction: Diane H. Felmlee, " 'Be Careful What You Wish for . . .': A Quantitative and Qualitative Investigation of *Fatal Attraction*," *Personal Relationships* 5 (1998), 235–53. Ximena B. Arriaga, "The Ups and Downs of Dating: Fluctuations in Satisfaction in Newly Formed Romantic Relationships," *Journal of Personality and Social Psychology* 80, no. 5 (2001), 754–65.

Fingers to the Bone: Bureau of Labor Statistics, "American Time Use Survey Summary," press release, June 25, 2008, http://www.bls.gov/news.release/atus.nr0.htm. Abbie E. Goldberg and Maureen Perry-Jenkins, "The Division of Labour and Perceptions of Parental Roles: Lesbian Couples Across the Transition to Parenthood," *Journal of Social and Personal Relationships* 24, no. 2 (2007); 297–319.

Merieke Van Willigen and Patricia Drentea, "Benefits of Equitable Relationships: The Impact of Sense of Fairness, Household Division of Labor, and Decision Making Power on Perceived Social Support," *Sex Roles* 44, no. 9–10 (2001), 571–97. Helen Couprie, "Time Allocation Within the Family: Welfare Implications of Life in a Couple," *Economic Journal* 117, no. 516 (2007), 287–305. Oriel Sullivan and Scott Coltrane, "Men's Changing Contribution to Housework and Childcare," a paper presented to the eleventh Annual Conference of the Council on Contemporary Families, 2008. Scott Coltrane, "Research on Household Labor: Modeling and Measuring the Social Embeddedness of Routine Family Work," *Journal of Marriage and Family* 62, no. 4 (2004), 1208–33. "Modern Marriage," Pew Research Center, http://pewresearch.org/pubs/542/modern-marriage.

Nag or Negotiate?: Diana Boxer, "Nagging: The Familial Conflict Arena," *Journal of Pragmatics* 34, no. 1 (2002), 49–61. Nadya A. Klinetob and David A. Smith, "Demand-Withdraw Communication in Marital Interaction: Tests of Interspousal Contingency and Gender Role Hypotheses," *Journal of Marriage and Family* 58, no. 4 (1996), 945–57. Tanya L. Chartrand, Amy N. Dalton, and Gavan Fitzsimons, "Nonconscious Relationship Reactance," *Journal of Experimental Social Psychology* 43, no. 5 (2007), 719–26.

Who Complains More?: Anita L. Vangelisti and John A. Daly, "Gender Differences in Standards for Romantic Relationships," *Personal Relationships* 4, no. 3 (1997), 203–19. Christine M. Proulx, Heather M. Helms, and C. Chris Payne, "Wives' Domain-specific 'Marriage Work' with Friends and Spouses: Links to Marital Quality," *Family Relations* 53, no. 4 (2004), 393–404.

One Too Many?: "Alcohol Problems in Intimate Relationships: Identification and Intervention," National Institute on Alcohol Abuse and Alcoholism, http://pubs.niaaa.nih.gov/publications/niaaa-guide/index.htm. Karim Dar, "Alcohol Use Disorders in Elderly People: Fact or Fiction?" *British Journal of Psychiatry* 12 (2006), 173–81. "Alcohol Misuse Among Older People," Alcohol Concern, http://www.alcoholconcern.org.uk/servlets/doc/50. Department of Health and Human Services, "Dietary Guidelines for Americans 2005," http://www.healthierus.gov/dietaryguidelines.

"We" Time: Ann C. Crouter, Matthew F. Bumpus, Melissa R. Head, and Susan M. McHale, "Implications of Overwork and Overload

for the Quality of Men's Family Relationships," *Journal of Marriage and Family* 63, no. 2 (2001), 404–16. Reg Gatenby, *Married Only at the Weekends? A Study of the Amount of Time Spent Together by Spouses* (London: Office for National Statistics, 2001). Marieke Voorpostel, "Spending Time Together—Changes in Joint Activities of Couples over Four Decades," August 2007, http://www.atususers.umd.edu/wip2/papers_i2007/Voorpostel.pdf. David Gray, "Congressional Testimony on the Challenges Facing American Workers," September 11, 2008, http://www.newamerica.net/publications/resources/2008/gray_testimony_house_ways_and_means. "Britain's Views on Family and Community," ICM poll for Equal Opportunity Commission, 2007. Thomas B. Holman and Mary Jacquart, "Leisure-activity Patterns and Marital Satisfaction: A Further Test," *Journal of Marriage and Family* 50, no. 1 (1988), 69–77. D. Donnelly, "Sexually Inactive Marriages," *Journal of Sex Research* 30, no. 2 (1993), 171–78.

Income-linked Divorce: Ithaca College, "Study Shows New Economy Puts Dual-income Couples in Double Jeopardy," press release, February 16, 2009, http://www.ithaca.edu/news/release.php?id=2631. Robert T. Brennan, Rosalind Chait Barnett, and Karen C. Gareis, "When She Earns More Than He Does: A Longitudinal Study of Dual-earner Couples," *Journal of Marriage and Family* 63, no. 1 (2001), 168–82. Stacy J. Rogers and Danelle D. DeBoer, "Changes in Wives' Income: Effects on Marital Happiness, Psychological Well-being, and the Risk of Divorce," *Journal of Marriage and Family* 63, no. 2 (2001), 458–72. D. Alex Heckert, Thomas C. Nowak, and K. A. Snyder, "The Impact of Husbands' and Wives' Relative Earnings on Marital Disruption," *Journal of Marriage and Family* 60, no. 3 (1998), 690–703. Fiona McAllister, "Effects of Changing Material Circumstances on the Incidence of Marital Breakdown," in One Plus One Marriage and Partnership Research, *High Divorce Rates: The State of the Evidence on Reasons and Remedies* (London: Family Policy Studies Unit, 1999).

Outlaw the In-laws?: M. Jean Turner, Carolyn R. Young, and Kelly I. Black, "Daughters-in-law and Mothers-in-law Seeking Their Place Within the Family: A Qualitative Study of Differing Viewpoints," *Family Relations* 55 (2006), 588–600. Chalandra M. Bryant, Rand D. Conger, and Jennifer M. Meehan, "The Influence of In-laws on

Change in Marital Success," *Journal of Marriage and Family* 63, no. 3 (2001), 614–26.

Pathetic Presents: Sandra L. Murray, John G. Holmes, Dale W. Griffin, Gina Bellavia, and Paul Rose, "The Mismeasure of Love: How Self-doubt Contaminates Relationship Beliefs," *Personality and Social Psychology Bulletin* 27, no. 4 (2001), 423–36. David J. Cheal, "The Social Dimensions of Gift Behavior," *Journal of Social and Personal Relationships* 3, no. 4 (1986), 423–39.

Question of Misery: Lisa Rauschmeier, "Coping Difficulty in Men Following Their Partner's Miscarriage: An Evolutionary Explanation," http://www.oswego.edu/~rauschme/evolutionary3.doc. Kristen M. Swanson, Zahra A. Karmali, Suzanne H. Powell, and Faina Pulvermakher, "Miscarriage Effects on Couples' Interpersonal and Sexual Relationships During the First Year After Loss: Women's Perceptions," *Psychosomatic Medicine* 65 (2003), 902–10. Manfred Beutel, Rainer Deckardt, Michael von Rad, and Herbert Weiner, "Grief and Depression After Miscarriage: Their Separation, Antecedents, and Course," *Psychosomatic Medicine* 57 (1995), 517–26. "Men and Miscarriage," Miscarriage Association, http://www.miscarriageassociation.org.uk/ma2006/information/leaflets/menmisc.pdf. Philip M. Boyce, John T. Condon, and David A. Ellwood, "Pregnancy Loss: A Major Life Event Affecting Emotional Health and Well Being," *Medical Journal of Australia* 178 (2002), 250–51. R. Neugebauer, J. Kline, A. Skodol, P. O'Connor, P. A. Geller, Z. Stein, and M. Susser, "Major Depressive Disorder in the 6 Months After Miscarriage," *Journal of the American Medical Association* 277, no. 5 (1997), 383–88.

Having Your Cake: Scott South and Kim Lloyd, "Spousal Alternatives and Marital Dissolution," *American Sociological Review* 60, no. 1 (1995), 21–36.

10. Happily Ever After

Not Just a Film: B. Wilson and S. Smallwood, "The Proportion of Marriages Ending in Divorce," *Popular Trends* 131 (2008), 28–36. Lawrence A. Kurdek, "The Nature and Predictors of the Trajectory of Change in Marital Quality for Husbands and Wives Over the First 10 Years of Marriage," *Developmental Psychology* 35, no. 5 (1999), 1283–96. Kelly Musick and Larry Bumpass, *Cohabitation,*

Marriage, and Trajectories in Well-being and Relationships (Los Angeles: California Center for Population Research, 2006). Kelly Musick and Larry Bumpass, Re-examining the Case of Marriage: Variation and Change in Well-being and Relationships (Los Angeles: California Center for Population Research, 2007). John Gottman and Clifford I. Notarius, "Decade Review: Observing Marital Interaction," Journal of Marriage and Family 62, no. 4 (2000), 862–79. Thomas N. Bradbury and Benjamin R. Karney, "Understanding and Altering the Longitudinal Course of Marriage," Journal of Marriage and Family 66 (2004), 862–79.

Leaving the Nest: Christine M. Proulx and Heather M. Helms, "Mothers' and Fathers' Perceptions of Change and Continuity in Their Relationships with Young Adult Sons and Daughters," Journal of Family Issues 29, no. 2 (2008), 234–61. L. Dennerstein, E. Dudley, and J. Guthrie, "Empty Nest or Revolving Door? A Prospective Study of Women's Quality of Life in Midlife During the Phase of Children Leaving and Re-entering the Home," Psychological Medicine 32 (2002), 545–50. Elizabeth Bates Harkins, "Effects of Empty Nest Transition on Self-Report of Psychological and Physical Well-Being," Journal of Marriage and Family 40, no. 3 (1978), 549–56. Bridget Hiedemann, Olga Suhomlinova, and Angela M. O'Rand, "Economic Independence, Economic Status, and Empty Nest in Midlife Marital Disruption," Journal of Marriage and Family 60, no. 1 (1998), 219–31.

Relationship Recovery: Marcus Eliason, "Lost Jobs, Broken Marriages," Working Papers of the Institute for Social and Economic Research, paper 2004–21. Lynda Clarke and Ann Berrington, "Socio-demographic Predictors of Divorce," in High Divorce Rates: The State of the Evidence on Reasons and Remedies, vol. 1, Lord Chancellor's Department, London, England.

Sofa So Good?: Kieran McKeown, Pauline Lehane, Trutz Haase, and Jonathan Pratschke, Unhappy Marriages: Does Counselling Help? (a report from ACCORD) (Dublin: Kieran McKeown, 2002). John Simons, "How Useful Is Relationship Therapy?" in High Divorce Rates: The State of the Evidence On Reasons and Remedies, vol. 2, Lord Chancellor's Department, London, England. Ilene Wolcott and Jody Hughes, "Towards Understanding the Reasons for Divorce," Working Paper no. 20, Australian Institute of Family Studies, 1999.

Remarriage Rush: Deborah Carr, "The Desire to Date and Remarry Among Older Widows and Widowers," *Journal of Marriage and Family* 66, no. 4 (2004), 1051–68. Kate Davidson, "Gender Differences in New Partnership Choices and Constraints for Older Widows and Widowers," *Ageing International* 27, no. 4 (2002), 43–60. Danielle Schneider, "Dating and Remarriage Over the First Two Years of Widowhood," *Annals of Clinical Psychiatry* 8, no. 2 (1996), 51–57. Zheng Wu and Christopher M. Schimmele, "Repartnering After First Union Disruption," *Journal of Marriage and Family* 67, no. 1 (2005), 27–36.

Menopausal Madness: Heather E. Dillaway, "Changing Menopausal Bodies: How Women Think and Act in the Face of a Reproductive Transition and Gendered Beauty Ideals," *Sex Roles* 53, no. 1–2 (2005), 1–17. Karen A. Matthews, "Myths and Realities of the Menopause," *Psychosomatic Medicine* 54, no. 1 (1992), 1–9. Louann Brizendine, *The Female Brain* (New York: Bantam Press, 2007).

Keeping Mum: Debra Umberson, "Marriage as Support or Strain? Marital Quality Following the Death of a Parent," *Journal of Marriage and Family* 57 (1995), 709–23. J. E. H. M. Hoekstra-Webers, J. P. C. Jaspers, W. A. Kamps, and E. C. Klip, "Marital Dissatisfaction, Psychological Distress, and the Coping of Parents of Pediatric Cancer Patients," *Journal of Marriage and Family* 60, no. 4 (1998), 1012–21.

Many Happy Retirements: *Aspects of Retirement for Older Women*, Australian Government Office for Women, 2006. Maximilliane E. Szinovacz and Adam Davey, "Retirement and Marital Decision Making: Effects on Retirement Satisfaction," *Journal of Marriage and Family* 67, no. 2 (2005), 387–98. National Institute on Aging, "Growing Older in America: The Health and Retirement Study," NIH publication no. 07-5757, March 2007, http://www.nia.nih.gov/Research Information/ExtramuralPrograms/BehavioralAndSocialResearch/ HRS.htm. David de Vaus and Yvonne Wells, "'I Married Him for Better or Worse but Not for Lunch': Retirement and Marriage," a paper presented to the eighth Australian Family Research Conference, Melbourne, Australia, 2003. Helen Barnes and Jane Parry, *Renegotiating Identity and Relationships: Men and Women's Adjustments to Retirement*, PSI Discussion Paper 14, Policy Studies Institute, 2003.

Ache of Hearts: Ilan S. Wittstein, David R. Thiermann, Joao A. C. Lima, Kenneth L. Baughman, Steven P. Shulman, et al., "Neurohumoral

Features of Myocardial Stunning Due to Sudden Emotional Stress," *New England Journal of Medicine* 352, no. 6 (2005), 539–48. C. Murray Parkes, R. Benjamin, and R. G. Fitzgerald, "Broken Heart: A Statistical Study of Increased Mortality Among Widowers," *British Medical Journal* 1 (1969), 740–43. Ilan S. Wittstein, "The Broken Heart Syndrome," *Cleveland Clinic Journal of Medicine* 74, suppl. 1 (2007), 17.

Everlasting Love: Nils Beckman, Magda Waern, Deborah Gustafson, and Ingmar Skoog, "Secular Trends in Self-reported Sexual Activity and Satisfaction in Swedish 70-year-olds: Cross-sectional Survey of Four Populations, 1971–2001," *British Medical Journal* 337 (2008), 279. F. Klagsbrun, *Married People: Staying Together in the Age of Divorce* (New York: Bantam Books, 1985). J. C. Lauer and R. H. Lauer, *'Til Death Do Us Part* (Binghamton, N.Y.: Haworth Press, 1986). John M. Gottman, Julie Schwartz Gottman, and Joan DeClaire, *10 Lessons to Transform Your Marriage* (New York: Three Rivers Press, 2006). Robyn Parker, *Why Marriages Last: A Discussion of the Literature* (Melbourne: Australian Institute of Family Studies, 2002). Robert W. Levenson, Laura L. Carstensen, and John M. Gottman, "Long-term Marriage: Age, Gender and Satisfaction," *Psychology and Aging* 8, no. 2 (1993), 301–13.

Index

About the Author

LUISA DILLNER, MD, is publishing director for new product development at the British Medical Journal Publishing Group. She has written for *The Guardian*, *The Observer*, *Sunday Telegraph*, *Cosmopolitan*, *Vogue*, and *Elle*. She has four children, lives in London, and, most important, has a perfect long-term relationship (only joking).